NICARAGUA

The Threat of a Good Example?

by Dianna Melrose

First published 1985

© OXFAM 1985

ISBN 0 85598 070 2

Printed by
Oxfam Print Room

Published by
OXFAM
274 Banbury Road
Oxford OX2 7DZ
United Kingdom

Acknowledgements

First and foremost I would like to thank all the Nicaraguan people who generously gave their time to help with research for this book, particularly Oxfam friends and project-holders who gave invaluable assistance. Our thanks also to individual members and officials of the following Nicaraguan organisations: AMNLAE (Nicaraguan Women's Association), CIDCA (Research and Documentation Centre for the Atlantic Coast), CIERA (Agrarian Reform Research and Study Centre), *Consejo Supremo Electoral* (Electoral Council), FACS (Augusto César Sandino Foundation), FIR (International Reconstruction Fund), Human Rights Commission, INSSBI (Institute of Social Security and Welfare), *La Prensa* Newspaper, the Ministries of Defence, Education, Finance, Health and the Interior; National Penitentiary System and UNAG (National Farmers' and Ranchers' Association).

I am very grateful to individuals and sister agencies in Europe and North America for their help, particularly CIIR (Catholic Institute for International Relations), Christian Aid, Nicaragua Solidarity Campaign, World University Service, Washington Office on Latin America, Institute for Policy Studies (Washington), Institute for Food and Development Policy (San Francisco), Lord Kennett and Oxfam Belgique. My thanks also to officials at the British Foreign and Commonwealth Office, Overseas Development Administration, Department of Trade and Industry, Export Credit Guarantee Department and at the Commission of the European Economic Community.

Finally, this book represents the collective experience of Oxfam field workers in Nicaragua over the past twenty years. It would never have materialised without the active collaboration of Oxfam colleagues in Managua, Mexico and Oxford.

Nicaragua

BELIZE

MEXICO

GUATEMALA

HONDURAS

EL SALVADOR

NICARAGUA

COSTA RICA

PANAMA

HONDURAS

RIVER COCO

Tasba Pri (Sumubila)

•Jalapa

Ocotal

NUEVA SEGOVIA

JINOTEGA

NORTH ZELAYA

Somoto

MADRIZ

•Condega

•Pantasma

•Waslala

Benjamin Zeledon

ESTELI

Potosi•

CHINANDEGA

•El Jicaro

MATAGALPA

LEON

Corinto

• Leon

BOACO

SOUTH ZELAYA

Puerto Sandino

MANAGUA

CHONTALES

El Bluff/ Bluefields

•Masaya

Lake Nicaragua

PACIFIC OCEAN

ATLANTIC OCEAN

RIO SAN JUAN

COSTA RICA

Contents

Introduction

SINCE THE OVERTHROW of the Somoza dictatorship in 1979 Nicaragua has attracted a great deal of polemic, much of it from people who have never been there. At one extreme is a media image of a Marxist-Leninist totalitarian State with close Soviet-Cuban links, that censors the press, persecutes minorities, and is involved in a massive arms build-up that threatens neighbouring countries. At the other extreme is Nicaragua as a Socialist Utopia.

Oxfam has worked in Nicaragua for more than 20 years. It is our experience of small-scale community development which we want to share in publishing this book. Our aim is also to give a voice to ordinary Nicaraguans. The aspirations of the poor are rarely newsworthy. Only when disaster strikes does attention focus on the poor. Then they emerge as victims, passively accepting their predicament. This stereotype could not be further from the truth, as the Nicaraguan people have shown.

Oxfam's goal worldwide is to support poor people in their efforts to improve their situation. This long-term development work is most likely to succeed where governments are genuinely committed to the needs of the poor majority. Rarely is this the case. Nicaragua stands out because of the positive climate for development based on people's active participation, which Oxfam has encountered over the past five years. Our experience is in no sense unique, but common to sister agencies in Britain and to voluntary agencies from many different countries.

This book traces the severe constraints on development work during the Somoza years, which raised doubts about whether to attempt to work in Nicaragua at all. Subsequently, since 1979 the scope for development has been enormous, with remarkable progress achieved in health, literacy and a more equitable distribution of resources.

Today, everyday life in Nicaragua is overshadowed by war. The *Contras* (or counter-revolutionary forces) are increasing their attacks on the civilian population from bases in Honduras and Costa Rica, with the declared aim of destabilising the elected Sandinista Government. This aggression is taking a daily toll in injury, homelessness and death. As documented in this book, the effects of the war on poor communities and development work are devastating.

Ordinary Nicaraguans are very conscious of the need for international support to help end the *Contra* war. For a British-based agency whose development work has been seriously disrupted by the fighting, this raises the key question of what more the British Government could be doing to help promote peace.

Nicaragua needs generous financial and development aid to help it out of serious economic crisis. We examine Britain's record in reducing aid to Nicaragua, despite the positive experience and requests for more funds from British voluntary agencies. We conclude that Britain could do far more to help stop the war and support development which offers real hope to the poor.

Chronology of Political Developments

1520s   Spanish conquest of Central America.

1620s   British begin trading with Indians on Nicaragua's Atlantic Coast.

1690s   British control over Atlantic Coast consolidated.

1821   Central American Federation gains independence from Spain.

1823   Monroe Doctrine claims the Americas as US sphere of influence.

1838   Nicaragua leaves Central America Federation to become autonomous republic.

1840s   Britain declares Mosquito Kingdom a British Protectorate.

1850   Clayton-Bulwer Treaty attempts to mediate between competing UK and US interests on Atlantic Coast and other parts of Central America.

1855   US filibuster William Walker comes to Nicaragua to back Liberals against Conservatives. Walker seizes power and reintroduces slavery, until deposed by Central American troops with British support.

1857   Beginning of 36 years uninterrupted Conservative rule and coffee boom.

1860   Anglo-Nicaraguan Treaty recognises Nicaraguan sovereignty on Atlantic Coast.

1893   Nationalist Liberal General José Santos Zelaya brought to power by new agro-exporting interests. Sixteen years of authoritarian modernization including separation of Church and State. Atlantic Coast incorporated into Nicaraguan territory. Zelaya's desire for an inter-oceanic canal through Nicaragua clashes with US plans to build Panama canal.

1909   Zelaya resigns after US-backed Conservative uprising. New Liberal President José Madriz unacceptable to US. Conservative employee of US company Aldolfo Diaz made President.

1912   Liberal General Benjamín Zelodón leads uprising against Conservatives. US marines land to crush revolt and remain in Nicaragua until 1925.

1914   Conservative President Chamorro signs Bryan-Chamorro treaty selling off territorial rights to USA, including right to construct canal.

1925   Unstable Conservative and Liberal coalition Government to power.

1926   US marines return to quell uprising led by Liberal General Moncada.

1927   Moncada agrees to surrender on US terms. Liberal officer Augusto César Sandino refuses to surrender and launches nationalist guerrilla offensive against US marines.

1932   US marines leave Nicaragua unable to defeat Sandino's guerrilla army; fighting left to US-trained National Guard under General Anastasio Somoza Garcia.

1933	Sandino accepts ceasefire, but his peace terms are unacceptable to Liberal President Sacasa and USA.
1934	Sandino assassinated by National Guard whilst leaving presidential palace.
1936	Anastasio Somoza seizes power from President Sacasa.
1956	President Somoza assassinated by poet Rigoberto Lopez Perez. Somoza's eldest son, Luis Somoza Debayle made President and younger son Anastasio Somoza Debayle becomes head of the National Guard.
1961	Carlos Fonseca Amador, Tomas Borge, Silvio Mayorga and others found the opposition FSLN (Sandinista Front for National Liberation) and begin clandestine organising and guerrilla attacks.
1967	Anastasio Somoza II assumes presidency after his brother's death.
1974	FSLN carries out successful Chema Castillo raid and releases hostages only after Somoza concedes to their demands. Guerrilla action continues.
1977	Opposition to dictatorship grows and support for FSLN voiced by new group of twelve prominent priests, intellectuals and business men — *Los Doce.*
1978	January: assassination of opposition newspaper editor Pedro Joaquin Chamorro, followed by strikes and widening opposition to Somoza. August: FSLN commando unit seizes National Palace and forces Somoza to release political prisoners. Strike called by broad opposition front. September: FSLN-led insurrection in major towns in north put down with massive repression and bombing by National Guard.
1979	Final offensive led by FSLN. Somoza flees on 17 July. National Guard surrender on 19 July. Government of National Reconstruction takes power.

1. The Somoza Era

"It doesn't take a band of revolutionaries to show people the deep injustices in their society. The poor generally know the source of their misery. What they lack is the power to change it."

J. Collins, with F. Moore Lappé & N. Allen, *What Difference Could a Revolution Make? Food and Farming in the New Nicaragua.*

NICARAGUA is similar in size to England and Wales, with a population of little more than three million. It is one of the six poorest countries in the whole of Latin America. As a crude indicator, income per head averaged US$920 in 1982, less than one tenth of average income in Britain that year.[1]

In common with the poor majority in other Central American countries, the Nicaraguan people have traditionally suffered from a flagrantly inequitable distribution of wealth and power. Poverty and inequality were deeply ingrained in Nicaraguan society during the rule of the Somoza family, which lasted from 1936 when the first Anastasio Somoza seized power, until his son was otherthrown in 1979.

Nicaragua has two distinct regions. The central coffee-growing highlands and coastal strip on the Pacific side where most of the population live, contrasts sharply with the sparsely-populated Atlantic coast which is mainly tropical rain-forest, swamp and pine savannah. There are also critical historical and cultural differences between the two regions, stemming largely from the fact that only the Pacific coast was colonised by Spain.

Mike Goldwater

The racial mix on Nicaragua's Atlantic coast — children of Spanish and African ancestry play together in the town of Bluefields.

4

The Miskitos and the Atlantic coast

Amongst the indigenous population of the Atlantic coast are the Miskitos and a smaller number of Sumu and Rama Indians. They were joined by immigrants from the English-speaking Caribbean and, more recently, by the numerically dominant Spanish-speaking migrants from the Pacific coast.

The separate development of the Atlantic coast was reinforced by bad communications and the lack of an all-weather road to link both parts of the country, a situation that continued throughout the Somoza era. By contrast, people on the Atlantic coast had a history of contact with the outside. During the colonial era, the British formed strategic alliances with Miskitos to protect their Caribbean commercial interests from the Spanish. Later, Britain intervened further in the Miskitos' affairs. From the 1840s the Mosquito Kingdom along the Atlantic coast became a British protectorate ruled by the Miskito king, with a British superintendent living in the Atlantic port of Bluefields.[2]

The United States was the next foreign power to become increasingly interested in Nicaragua as a potential site for a canal to link the Atlantic and Pacific oceans. The Atlantic coast attracted particular attention from American lumber and banana interests. During the 19th Century, these US companies acquired large concessions in the region's natural resources and drew the Miskitos into waged labour in their gold and silver mines, in lumbering and on the banana plantations.

But the foreign investors began pulling out, first as a result of the 1930s banana plague, then once hardwoods and pine became depleted in the 1950s. The mining industry was allowed to run down and overfishing also contributed to the region's decline. Miskitos who had long since abandoned their traditional livelihood for waged labour were left stranded. Their plight was completely ignored at home and abroad.

In 1960, the lives of Miskito communities were disrupted as a result of an International Court of Justice ruling, which was designed to settle a longstanding territorial dispute between Honduras and Nicaragua. The new frontier was set along the River Coco. This effectively carved the Miskitos' homelands in two and meant that they had to choose either Nicaraguan or Honduran citizenship. Several thousand who opted to live in Nicaragua were then stopped from growing crops on the Honduran side of the River Coco, as they had done for generations. They were resettled by the Nicaraguan Government, but the nearest fertile land was seven miles away and totally inadequate for their needs. They were left to fend for themselves without financial or technical help to get food production started.

It was in response to the needs of these displaced Miskitos that Oxfam began work in Nicaragua in 1964, with a small grant of just over £1,000. This covered the cost of one hundred machetes and fifty axes to enable the Miskitos to clear the virgin land for planting, and a small truck to transport the cassava they produced back to the settlement.[3]

The amount of money involved in this and later grants was very small. But to the Miskitos its significance lay in an awareness that, at last, the outside world was beginning to take an interest in their situation. Later support included more equipment for the agricultural cooperative they set up, a loan to buy coconut saplings and, after a severe hurricane in 1971, a loan for seeds to the Tasba Raya community.[4]

For Oxfam, this initial contact with the Miskitos marked the beginning of a longstanding concern for the development problems affecting people on the Atlantic coast. The initial focus of longer-term development work, begun in the early 1970s, was health. Poverty-related diseases were prevalent throughout Nicaragua, and there were serious outbreaks of infectious disease, such as the 1967 polio epidemic.[5] But on the Atlantic coast, the problems were magnified: the tuberculosis incidence, for example, was four times the national average, and an estimated 80% of people suffered from internal parasites and malaria. In response to this situation, a preventive health and leadership training programme was set up with Miskito and Sumu communities along the River Coco.[6]

The 1972 earthquake

Before dawn on Christmas Eve 1972, a massive earthquake shook Managua. It killed up to 20,000 people, left thousands more homeless and the city centre in ruins. In Britain a joint agency disaster appeal was launched, which raised about £400,000. Of necessity, the focus of Oxfam's programme switched to the Pacific coast.

The Managua earthquake was to provide new insights into poverty and corruption under Somoza. In the immediate aftermath of the earthquake, Somoza's National Guard went on the rampage looting and stealing. A National Emergency Committee, set up under President Somoza's control and run by the National Guard, institutionalised the misappropriation of

Jenny Matthews

Collecting water in Managua in the zone known as *Los Escombros* (the ruins), once the heart of the city but devastated by the 1972 earthquake.

emergency relief. Realising that relief supplies were being syphoned off and sold by the National Guard, Oxfam's Field Director talked Mrs Somoza into giving permission to bypass the official distribution system. This meant waiting in the air traffic control tower for the right plane to be spotted, then careering onto the tarmac to get the trucks loaded before the National Guard arrived on the scene.

Huge tents imported in this way were used to set up improvised community centres for food distribution and health care. Special camp committees were formed to run the centres. But these attempts by the earthquake victims to organise themselves were later broken up by the National Guard.[7]

Ironically, the earthquake which destroyed Managua's commercial centre, causing millions of pounds' worth of damage, was to turn the Nicaraguan economy into the fastest-growing in the region. This was made possible by the massive inflow of funds for reconstruction. It enabled the Somozas to extend their interests into construction and property, making them the single main beneficiary. By contrast, the urban poor, who were hit hardest by the earthquake, now faced increasing hardship. The housing situation became more precarious for the poor as speculators moved in and the rents shot up. Many families became embroiled in protracted legal battles over land that remained unresolved until 1979.[8]

Land expropriation

These land disputes in and around Managua were symptomatic of the key problem confronting peasant farmers throughout Nicaragua. The majority desperately needed land. Yet during the late 1970s, an estimated 30% of the best land on the big estates was left completely idle, or inadequately used.[9]

Through a gradual process of land concentration, peasant farmers on the Pacific coast had been pushed off good land by the big landowners who wanted to expand production of cotton, sugar and beef for export. The peasant farmers had been forced onto less fertile, virgin land which had to be cleared before they could grow maize, beans and other food crops. For survival, many landless peasants and others with land too poor to feed their families, had no option but to look for badly-paid seasonal work on the big estates. They had to migrate with the coffee, cotton and sugar harvests, and only a minority were guaranteed regular wages outside the months of peak demand for labour.

Peasant farmers who resisted expulsion risked being burnt out by the National Guard, who protected the interests of the large landowners. National Guard officers, Somoza included, made personal fortunes from export crops, particularly cotton. Peasant families responded by organising land invasions, which were widespread in the provinces of León and Chinandega. Some were successful, but most failed.

In August 1976, a group of 600 people were successful in taking over idle land on a large estate at Los Arcos, in the department of León. They planted crops and were joined by eight more families who took over some adjoining land. These peasant farmers organised themselves into a cooperative, with help from a small voluntary agency for community development and the Legal Aid Service of León University.[10] Within a year they had built over 50 houses and a communal building that they used as as school, church and weekly clinic.

The families faced severe problems including harassment from the absentee landowner. But the whole experience of organising themselves, and taking joint decisions to increase production and set up a clinic, all created confidence in their own abilities and in what might be achieved in Nicaragua without Somoza.

The experience of the cooperative at Los Arcos was not unique. Throughout the country poor people were coming together and forming peasant associations, trades unions, neighbourhood and women's groups. They began working together on small-scale community efforts to improve health, literacy and food production. But the community leaders and others involved all ran high risks.

Obstacles to community development

By 1972 reports were coming in of murder and violence targeted against local community leaders. Their efforts at organising people to improve their situation were seen as a threat to the Government-sponsored community development organisation, *Prodesarollo.* As the political and military power of the opposition to Somoza grew, repression became less selective, more brutal and more widespread.

Opponents of the dictatorship had come together in the early sixties to form the Sandinista Front for National Liberation (FSLN). The Front took its inspiration from General Augusto César Sandino who led a nationalist uprising in the early 1930s against the US marines and Nicaraguan Government,

Dianna Melrose

"Sandino Lives" — graffiti in Ocotal, 1984. Augusto César Sandino, who led a nationalist uprising against Government forces and the US marines in the early 1930s, is the national hero to whom opponents of the Somoza dictatorship looked for inspiration.

which he saw as having sold out to US economic interests. Sandino's guerrilla army drew widespread support from peasants in the north and central highlands, where they organised cooperatives and literacy classes. In 1934, Sandino was ambushed and killed by the National Guard, then under the command of the future first President Somoza. After Sandino's assassination, a campaign of terror was unleashed in the provinces where his support was strongest. Peasants were butchered and the cooperatives destroyed.

Forty years later, in the mid-1970s, violence and fear of the National Guard continued unabated. Merely participating in a meeting or community initiative was sufficient for people to be dealt with as 'Communists'. Attendance at evening classes fell because people were afraid to go out at night. Secret police infiltrated cooperative meetings to tape-record conversations or break them up. After the Roman Catholic bishops denounced systematic terror and extermination, pressures against church groups mounted and foreign priests were threatened with cancellation of their residence visas.[11]

Increased guerrilla activity in the northern Jalapa region resulted in fierce repression by the National Guard. Members of CEDECO, an Oxfam-supported community development group in Jalapa, found it impossible to move around to carry out their work.[12] Finally the team had to flee the country, along with many more cooperative members and Oxfam project holders. They joined the 10,000 or so refugees in camps in Honduras, to whom emergency food and medicines were supplied.[13]

The systematic violation of human rights was carefully documented by the National Youth Movement's legal aid centre, originally set up to help those made homeless by the 1972 earthquake.[14] Subsequently, they ran legal training courses for cooperative leaders, community workers and trades unionists, who faced constant harassment from the authorities, and tried to help the growing number of political prisoners.

People organised themselves into neighbourhood committees to protect themselves from the brutal repression perpetrated by the National Guard. It was the mass of ordinary men, women and children who took to the streets to call for Somoza's resignation, especially in 1978 after the assassination of the La Prensa newspaper editor, Pedro Joaquín Chamorro. They were joined by middle class and better-off Nicaraguans who were all suffering the stifling effects of the dictatorship on political, social and economic life. Finally, in July 1979, it was a very broad-based coalition of urban and rural people that toppled Somoza under the leadership of the Sandinistas.

The overthrow of the Somoza dictatorship was achieved only at enormous cost in human suffering. An estimated 50,000 people, almost 2% of the population, died in the process — the equivalent proportionately in Britain to the entire population of the City of Birmingham.[15] Factories, schools and hospitals were destroyed in bombing raids by the National Guard. Homes were ruined and some 45,000 children left as orphans.

This tragic loss of life was compounded by the deaths of the natural leaders of many communities which had to set about the task of reconstruction without them. The legacy of abject poverty left by the dictatorship (see over) presented an enormous challenge to the Nicaraguan people and their new Government. After decades of severe constraints on meaningful development, the potential was there to begin to tackle the roots of poverty on a national scale.

Dianna Melrose

"The past will never return" Ocotal, 1984 — the writing on the wall is indicative of all the bad memories of poverty and suffering during the Somoza years. Ocotal, a town near the Honduran border, was occupied by the *Contra* during June 1984.

THE SOMOZA LEGACY

— One baby in eight under one year old died, compared with one in eighty-three in Britain.

— Two out of three children under five were undernourished.

— 93% of rural homes had no safe drinking water.

— Six out of ten deaths were caused by preventable and curable diseases.

— Over half the population was illiterate.

— The poorest 50% of Nicaraguans received 15% of national income; the richest 5% almost twice as much.

— Two out of three peasant farmers were completely landless or had plots too small to meet their basic needs.

— Export crops took up 90% of agricultural credit and 22 times more arable land than land used to grow basic food crops.

— 20% unemployment in Managua and only 60% of working people on regular wages in the poorest districts.

— 90% of medical services catering for only 10% of the population, with more than half the country's doctors clustered in the capital city.

— Less than 20% of under-fives and pregnant women were receiving health care.

— 94% of rural children were unable to finish even primary school.

Sources

Nicaraguan Health Ministry, UNICEF, *New England Journal of Medicine* (5 August 1982), Instituto Histórico Centroamericano, Institute for Food and Development Policy.

2. A New Start for the People

"What we see is a government faced with tremendous problems, some seemingly insuperable, bent on a great experiment which, though precarious and incomplete at many points, provides hope to the poor sectors of society, improves the conditions of education, literacy and health, and for the first time offers the Nicaraguan people a modicum of justice for all rather than a society offering privilege exclusively to the wealthy . . . and to the powerful." World Council of Churches, *Report on Nicaragua,* 1983.

"IN FIVE YEARS we amaze ourselves with what we've achieved. Now we've got land and we can get credit. We've planted maize, sorghum, rice and beans. We have an irrigation scheme and calves we're fattening. Before, things were very bad. The National Guard took our land for the big owners and the banks wouldn't lend us anything." The pride of this 48-year-old member of the Pedro Altamirano cooperative, near León, is typical of thousands of small farmers who, of all Nicaraguans, have probably participated in the most dramatic changes since July 1979.

Dianna Melrose

Daisy Guevara and one of her children in the new school that the local community has built. This doubles up as a primary school and adult education centre.

Daisy Guevara, who makes her living selling iced drinks to workers on another cooperative near the El Limón mine, persuades us to go and see the school she and her neighbours have built. The children go to the school in the daytime, in the evening it is an adult education centre. Now a neighbour's daughter has trained to be their health promoter, or *brigadista*. They still have lots of problems, especially with transport. Some days, Daisy has to wait five or six hours for a lift from the main road. But, like many Nicaraguans who had so little in the past, Daisy's enthusiasm for what they have now is infectious.

Of course, there are dissenting voices, particularly amongst the better-off, but also amongst the poor. An elderly woman in a poor neighbourhood of Managua complains bitterly about soaring food prices. The family used to eat beef. Now on the few occasions they can afford to buy meat, it is mainly gristle. The imported beans in the market are tasteless, nothing like the delicious red *frijolitos* they used to sell. She criticises the Government at the top of her voice, undeterred by the stream of passers-by.

The social advances that have benefited the poor majority, increasingly serious food shortages, and underlying economic crisis are all part of the reality of Nicaragua today. The problems are partly symptomatic of the huge obstacles to breaking with the past and pursuing far-reaching social, political and economic change.

After what Nicaraguans call the 'triumph' on 19 July 1979 when the old Government fell, rapid changes were set in motion. However, from Oxfam's perspective, there was a strong element of continuity. Many dedicated individuals, whom Oxfam had come to know and trust through their involvement in small-scale community development, now held senior positions in the Ministries of Agrarian Reform, Education, Health and Social Security. Their practical experience of the problems and their commitment to improving the lives of ordinary people were to be crucial in shaping the new national priorities.

The cornerstone of the new development strategy, spelled out by the Sandinista Front some years before taking power, was to give priority to meeting the basic needs of the poor majority. This was to be achieved by involving people in implementing change at a local level, through their neighbourhood groups, peasant associations and other organisations; at a central level, representatives of these organisations were to cooperate closely with the Government Ministries.

The new Government of National Reconstruction stressed its desire to develop a mixed economy and political pluralism in a country that had no tradition of democracy or free elections. Great importance was also attached to achieving a high degree of national self-sufficiency and an independent, non-aligned foreign policy.

This radically new focus of social policy in Nicaragua towards the needs of the poor presented enormous scope for Oxfam's work. In addition to locally-based projects, Oxfam was now able to support nationwide initiatives to tackle problems rooted in poverty. The concept of actively involving people in development through community organisations is neither new nor radical, but widely recognised to be a precondition for successful development.[1] How-

The 1980 Literacy Crusade. Workers learning basic literacy skills at La Cruz near Managua.

ever, as the World Bank points out: "Governments . . . vary greatly in the commitment of their political leadership to improving the condition of the people and encouraging their active participation in the development process".[2] From Oxfam's experience of working in seventy-six developing countries, Nicaragua was to prove exceptional in the strength of that Government commitment.

The Literacy Crusade

"We believe that in order to create a new nation we have to begin with an education that liberates people. Only through understanding their past and their present, only through understanding and analysing their reality can people choose their future." Fernando Cardenal, National Coordinator for the Literacy Crusade and Education Minister from 1984.

When the Government of National Reconstruction took power, less than half the Nicaraguan people over the age of ten could read or write. The national average masked greater inequalities, particularly in the rural areas. In some villages all the women and the majority of men were illiterate because there had been no local school, and secondary education had been the preserve of a privileged minority.

The sheer numbers of illiterate people presented a major obstacle to the new Government in successfully communicating its plans and encouraging people to participate in decisions affecting their lives. The problems were compounded by people's lack of experience of community organisation and political debate. Decades of dictatorship and anti-Communist propaganda had created fear and mistrust in the minds of many people. The relative isolation of the Atlantic coast, which had been spared the worst excesses of the dictatorship, meant that many of its people saw the revolution as all to do with the 'Spanish' and completely alien to their lives. These geographical and linguistic barriers presented added complications to tackling illiteracy.

Planning for a national literacy campaign was under way well in advance of July 1979. In the post-Somoza euphoria it was presented as a national crusade against one of the worst legacies of the dictatorship. The campaign was launched in March 1980, this timing having been carefully planned not to clash with the peak harvest season from November to March when people would be too busy to take part. Because of the huge numbers to be taught and the shortage of resources, the campaign revolved around 95,000 volunteers who came forward to be trained to teach basic literacy skills. These *brigadistas* were mostly secondary and college students who were to leave the towns to teach in the rural areas. Factory workers, civil servants and professional people, amongst them a high percentage of women, volunteered to run evening classes in the poorer urban neighbourhoods.

Preparation and training lasted six months, starting with a pilot project which involved 80 volunteers in testing the teaching materials and methodology. This was followed by an intensive course for 560 literacy teachers; they trained 7,000 *brigadistas* who, in their turn, went on to prepare the rest, so that all 95,000 were covered.[3] This multiplier approach to training had been used before in Nicaragua on a much smaller scale. But nothing on the revolutionary scale of the Literacy Crusade had been attempted before in Latin America.

A national literacy census taken at the beginning of 1980 was used to identify the numbers and whereabouts of likely participants. Local people were actively encouraged to join the literacy classes by the neighbourhood groups, the National Women's Association and individual unions, such as the Agricultural Workers' Association and Teachers' Union. Each department had a literacy committee responsible for allocating the *brigadistas* to different local communities and organising their accommodation and food. The committees also distributed paper, pencils, blackboards and textbooks and were to monitor progress.

The launch of the campaign excited a great deal of public interest, and many offers of practical support. Owners of lorries and buses lent their vehicles to transport the *brigadistas*, donations were made to pay for their uniforms and many people worked overtime, standing in for colleagues absent because of the campaign.

The plan was to take literacy skills *to* the people by holding lessons in their homes and communities to minimise demands on their time and the disruption and expense of having to travel to evening classes. Teaching materials had been designed to be of immediate relevance to people's lives and to explain the Sandinistas' policies in the context of Nicaraguan history, and especially the role of the nationalist hero, Sandino.

But the campaign was seen as very much a two-way process. By living in the homes of peasant families and working alongside them in the fields, the young, urban, and mostly middle class *brigadistas* would acquire new practical skills and a better understanding of the social and economic reality of most

Nicaraguans. For many, it was their first insight into the hard physical life in the rural areas, and an opportunity to absorb cultural traditions that had been increasingly eclipsed in the cities by imported culture.

By the official end of the six-month Literacy Crusade in August 1980, over 400,000 Nicaraguans had learnt some basic literacy skills. On the Atlantic coast about 12,000 people had been able to learn some reading and writing in Miskito, Suma and English, with specially prepared materials. The immense voluntary effort of the *brigadistas*, community organisers and local people resulted in a fall in the national rate of illiteracy from 53% to 13%. This was achieved with a budget of only 12 million dollars, in contrast with the experience of other Latin American countries, where bigger budgets had achieved much less. The success of the campaign won international recognition and the 1980 UNESCO Literacy Prize.[4]

Adult education

Since the majority of students could realistically only achieve very basic literacy in such a short period, an Adult Education Programme was subsequently set up to give people the opportunity to build on their new skills. This programme was modelled on the community-based approach of the Literacy Crusade, with popular education collectives established in 17,000 communities. It was conceived as a two-stage programme. The first two years allowed students to catch up on the primary school curriculum and the second two years focused more on occupational and practical skills.[5]

With the impetus of the Literacy Crusade behind it, the Adult Education Programme got off to a good start but subsequently lost momentum. The Programme was left under-resourced as Government and agency funding shifted to new priority areas. The rural population was also asked to give priority to agricultural production and was increasingly taken up with defence against *Contra* attacks. The 'popular teachers' who ran the course were local people, many of whom had themselves only completed two or three years of primary school, which left them inadequately trained for the demands made on them.

Oxfam supported both the Literacy Crusade and the Adult Education Programme in Boaco province, traditionally one of the most backward areas in terms of education.[6] Between 1979 and 1981 the illiteracy rate was successfully halved. But, at 33%, it remained twice the national average. This reflects the acute lack of education facilities inherited from the Somoza regime. In 1979, Boaco had the smallest number of primary schools covering all four grades in the country. By contrast, the province had a particularly good network of all-weather roads built to serve the large cattle estates owned by Somoza and his associates.[7]

New schools

Somoza's Government had shown great reluctance to build new schools, to the point that Oxfam project-holders running the legal aid centre of the National Youth Movement had had to organise petitions to the Ministry of Education on behalf of poor communities which urgently wanted a school.[8]

Nicaragua is a young society, with half its population under 15. This presents a major challenge for a poor country with very limited resources. But the

Jenny Matthews

Healthy babies at a Government crêche for children of tobacco factory workers in Esteli. Pre-school facilities which were the preserve of a fee-paying minority before 1979 are now available free to many working class parents.

Government of National Reconstruction took responsibility for giving all Nicaraguans the right to education. The expansion of primary education between 1979 and 1984 was dramatic. There are now 127% more schools, 61% more teachers and 55% more children at primary school. With the organised participation of local people, 1,404 new schools have been built, 95% of them in rural areas.[9] The Government provides the building materials and technical advice, and in many cases local people have taken on responsibility for building and organising their new school.

Altogether there has been a five-fold increase in resources allocated to education since 1978, including a substantial expansion in secondary education and schools for children with special learning difficulties. Pre-school facilities — which in 1978 were only available to about 9,000 young children mostly in private fee-paying schools — now cover about 70,000 under-sixes, mainly in free day-care centres run by the Social Welfare Ministry.[10]

Attempts have been made to establish broad-based consultation over education policy. Early in 1981, in drawing up new education principles the Ministry of Education consulted over 50,000 people, including members of 30 different union, church, community and political organisations. But the formal structures for participatory decision-making have been under-used, both because of organisational weakness and all the different issues requiring the attention of the mass organisations.

Public health

"In just three years, more has been done in most areas of social welfare than in fifty years of dictatorship under the Somoza family." *The New England Journal of Medicine,* 5.2.82.

The appalling state of health resulting from decades of poverty and inadequate health services, required concerted Government and community action. Malaria, tuberculosis and internal parasites were endemic in much of the country. One in three Nicaraguans suffered at least one malaria attack during their life. The top ten killer diseases of young children were preventable and treatable: tetanus, measles, whooping cough and dehydration from diarrhoea all contributed to very high child death rates. In many cases the underlying problem was hunger. Studies showed that in some areas up to 83% of Nicaraguan children were malnourished, and the proportion of severely malnourished children could be as high as 45%.[11]

The Literacy Crusade had demonstrated the effectiveness of mobilising people to tackle a specific problem. Based on this experience a series of nationwide public health campaigns was launched to eradicate the major infectious diseases. These 'Popular Health Days' (*Jornadas Populares de Salud*) were planned and coordinated nationally by the Popular Health Council. This included representatives from the Ministry of Health and the mass organisations such as the Agricultural Workers' Union, the Women's Association and the neighbourhood groups.

At local and departmental levels, similar representative committees were responsible for implementing national plans and selecting local people to be trained as community health promoters, or *brigadistas*. During the 1982 public health campaign to clean up the streets and neighbourhoods, a total of 4,700 'multipliers' were trained. They went on to train 30,000 *brigadistas* (mainly young local people, over half of them women) who successfully mobilised local people into burning rubbish and draining stagnant water.[12] Because of Oxfam's long-standing involvement in health work on the Atlantic coast, the organisation contributed US$100,000 to the cost of the 1982 public health campaigns in North Zelaya.[13]

The Popular Health Days have achieved some impressive results. During

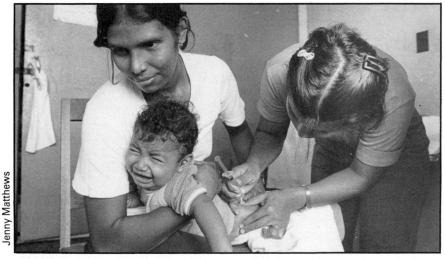

Vaccination coverage of babies under a year old is impressive even in comparison with developed countries like Britain.

one of the first campaigns in 1981, over half a million under-fives were innoculated against polio and measles. In the following two years, not a single case of polio was reported, and measles dropped from being the fifth most common infectious disease to the thirteenth. Similarly, a three-pronged attack against malaria launched that year resulted in a 98% fall in new malaria cases.[14] The three elements were: community action to fill in ditches where mosquitoes breed, chemical spraying, and a three-day course of the anti-malaria drugs chloroquine and primaquine. The *brigadistas* administered these drugs to 1.9 million people (about 70% of the population), a coverage described by a British expert as "an extraordinary achievement".[15]

Whereas it is estimated that in 1979 little more than quarter of the population could obtain medical services, by 1982 about 70% of Nicaraguans had regular access to health care.[16] In the process, there was a radical shift from primarily curative, urban-based care for a privileged minority to an emphasis on prevention, which is particularly striking in the area of maternal and child care.

Vaccination coverage of babies under a year old is impressive — even in comparison with developed countries like Britain — with 88% immunised against polio and 78% against measles in 1983.[17] To prevent infant deaths from dehydration caused by diarrhoea, 360 special rehydration units have been set up around the country, backed by the *brigadistas* who make home visits and explain the importance of fluids. The Nicaraguan Government has also been active in alerting mothers to the possible hazards of bottle-feeding. Advertising of infant formula has been banned and mothers are urged to breastfeed.

Special courses for traditional midwives, who assist at well over half of all births, were started in Matagalpa and Jinotega, in the north of the country. These aimed to build on the midwives' empirical knowledge and help to reduce the risk of neo-natal tetanus. The training has become popular with midwives right across the northern border zone. For many women the courses and the 'graduation' ceremony at which they are each presented with a special midwife's kit, means that for the first time their skills and services are acknowledged as important and appreciated beyond their immediate community.[18]

Miners' health

Since 1979 action has been taken to improve workers' health through safer working conditions and controlling toxic hazards, such as pesticides. Health problems affecting miners were particularly acute. On the Atlantic coast, an estimated 90% of the Miskito miners were suffering from silicosis.[19] On the Pacific coast, at the El Limón gold and silver mine which was founded by Cornishmen in the 1860s, one in three miners was found to be suffering from pneumoconiosis, a preventable lung disease caused by inhaling high levels of dust. Before the mine was nationalised in 1979, its Canadian owners had made only minimal investments in health and safety. Miners had to work long shifts in poorly ventilated shafts in unbearable temperatures that could be as high as 60°C.

Miners at the El Limón gold mine, near León, wearing new helmets sent from Britain. Before the mine was nationalised in 1979 these miners had to work long shifts in poorly ventilated shafts in temperatures as high as 60°C. One in three was suffering from pneumoconiosis before measures were taken to improve health and safety in the mine.

Now, with improved ventilation and planning by 22 technicians including a British CIIR volunteer (as opposed to just two before 1979), only the hottest shafts reach over 40°C. New machinery has helped to reduce dust, but some is inevitable so miners have recently been provided with protective masks, as well as new boots, helmets and overalls from Britain.[20]

Land reform

Nicaragua is primarily an agricultural society, with the majority of its workforce involved in some aspect of agricultural production or distribution. Production had been badly disrupted during the war to oust Somoza, leading to serious food shortages and a sharp fall in export earnings. In July 1979, an immediate national priority was to reactivate food production and begin to tackle some of the structural problems in the rural areas. Up to a third of arable land, mainly on large estates, was idle or under-used, whilst the majority of peasant farmers were clamouring for land.[21]

Land abandoned by Somoza and his associates who had fled abroad was immediately expropriated and converted into State farms and peasant cooperatives. On an area of confiscated land in Managua, the Chilote project was set up to provide some 150 jobs at a time of high unemployment and serious food shortages. Maize and vegetables were planted with Oxfam support for this and the subsequent *Don Frijol* project to produce kidney beans and rice.[22] Half the profit made was kept for a revolving fund to pay for future production. The remainder was to be used for community services, starting with a local store that would sell basic food items at low prices, which served to

Jenny Matthews

strengthen the local neighbourhood groups.

The objectives of these small-scale initiatives were complementary to the 1980 national 'Emergency Economic Plan to Benefit the People', which aimed to boost agricultural production and basic food consumption, create 95,000 new jobs, reduce inflation from 60% to 22%, and strengthen the new cooperatives being set up on expropriated land. The mass organisations, particularly the Agricultural Workers' Association (ATC) were active in implementing the plan. In the key cotton and sugar-producing department of Chinandega, for example, the ATC organised 50 three-day training workshops for its 17,000 members and was active in recruiting new members on the big private estates which had not previously been unionised.[23] This enabled the badly-paid labourers to negotiate for better pay and conditions.

Meanwhile, small peasant farmers for whom the revolution had primarily held out the promise of land, waited impatiently for land reform. In the event, the Agrarian Reform Law was not enacted until July 1981, by which time many peasant families had spontaneously taken over idle land. The criteria behind the agrarian reform were to make the land as productive as possible without imposing any limit on the size of private land-holdings, and owners were to be compensated for expropriated land. This pragmatic reform underlined the Government's commitment to a mixed economy, whilst acknowledging the vital importance of large private producers to the export sector. These big estates produced 72% of national cotton, 58% of beef, 53% of coffee and 51% of sugar, four products which alone netted two-thirds of total export earnings in 1978.[24]

The main beneficiaries from land reform and a five-fold increase in State credit between 1979 and 1982 were peasant farmers. Between October 1981 and August 1984, 49,661 families received titles to land.[25] Titles were given free but could not be sold, to prevent possible renewed land concentration or fragmentation into uneconomic plots. Peasant farmers were encouraged to

Rural workers from cooperatives receive their land titles at a ceremony in August 1983 in Masaya.

21

After the maize harvest at the Oxfam-supported Pedro Altamirano Cooperative near León.

form cooperatives by being given priority in the allocation of land and better credit terms.

New cooperatives

The expansion of cooperatives is seen as an important strategy for increasing food production for home consumption. It is easier for government ministries to provide services, credit, technical know-how and agricultural inputs to organised cooperatives than to isolated peasant farmers.

Because of the importance of small and medium-size farmers to basic food production, a new national association (UNAG) was formed in 1981 to represent them. This gave impetus to the formation of cooperatives. By 1983, more than half the country's small and medium producers had joined either a cooperative in which members share credit and services but work their own land, or one in which land is also worked cooperatively.[26]

Local UNAG representatives work closely with the cooperatives and help members to plan production and marketing. Because of the acute shortage of technical advisers, UNAG has concentrated resources on some of the more successful cooperatives to serve as demonstration models for neighbouring cooperatives. One of these is the Pedro Altamirano cooperative, near León, which produces maize, sorghum, rice and beans. Its 22 members were doing well until their crops were devastated by serious flooding in 1982. The Government covered the cooperative's immediate losses and Oxfam, with EEC co-funding, provided money for a revolving fund which the cooperative used to buy 120 calves for fattening.[27]

Food production

Nicaragua's small and medium farmers now produce over three-quarters of the food for home consumption and just over 40% of export crops. To some extent they have benefited from the guaranteed prices that the new State buying agency ENABAS offers. Results in meeting national production targets over the past five years have been a mixture of success and some failures. Overall agricultural production increased by 8% between 1979 and 1983.[28]

The most impressive increases have been in the production of sorghum, rice, chicken, eggs and pork. Kidney bean yields are up, but have been very unstable. Production of bananas, potatoes, cassava, tomatoes and cabbage have all increased since 1980, and the volume of sugar and coffee exports in 1983 was well up on 1977.[29] The main production failures, on the other hand, have been maize, cotton, beef and milk. In the case of beef, 200,000 cattle were estimated to have been rustled over the Honduran border by mid-1981 in an attempt to remove capital assets. Similarly cotton has yet to recover from the effects of the civil war, decapitalisation and the severe 1982 floods in the main cotton-producing region.

Some of the production failures can be traced to counter-productive Government pricing policies and a tendency for stop-gap measures and price increases that come too late. At a regional UNAG meeting in the northern town in Ocotal in September 1984, representatives from cooperatives criticised the Government for having priced maize and beans so low that there was no incentive to produce them, in comparison with the relatively good returns on coffee and cotton. They also complained of delays in processing credit applications, inadequate technical assistance and profiteering by middlemen.

Nicaragua is still having to import basic foods because of the combined effects of increased demand and production shortfalls. Large quantities of milk powder are being imported, together with wheat, for which a local demand has been created that cannot be satisfied by local production.

"From zero to 15 thousand pounds of pork a day — 98% property of the people." Billboard in Managua, April 1982. Production and consumption of pork, chicken, eggs, rice and other foods increased significantly by 1982. But there have been production failures too and nutritional gains are increasingly threatened by the *Contra* war and economic crisis.

Consumption of basic foods

Increased production alone could not have ensured better nutrition for the poor, especially when middlemen have been quick to exploit production shortfalls and charge exorbitant prices. It was thus a significant achievement that between 1976/78 and 1980/82, per capita consumption of the majority of basic foods increased.[30] The exceptions (largely attributable to production failures) included consumption of maize, milk and beef which slumped. As a result, people in the urban areas who, under Somoza could get beef provided they had the money to pay for it, now find it in very short supply and are highly critical of the food situation.

But for the majority of the rural poor there have been marked improvements because food is more equitably distributed around the country. Products like cooking oil, rice, chicken, eggs and sugar, previously very scarce in rural areas, are now far more widely consumed by the poor majority. This has been made possible by Government subsidies and strict controls on prices and distribution of basic food items. Special distribution outlets were set up for eight basic commodities: rice, beans, maize, flour, sugar, salt, cooking oil and soap. More recently, distribution of these basic items through the neighbourhood groups has been tightened up to protect the interests of the poorest at a time of growing shortages and rising prices.

Loss of fear

Besides the physical improvements in people's lives through better nutrition, health care and community services, another major change for those who lived through the Somoza years has been the loss of fear. In July 1979, one of the new Government's first acts was to abolish the death penalty and set out citizens' basic rights. As a result, thousands of Nicaraguans who had suffered the institutionalised violence of the National Guard under Somoza, found that for the very first time they could live without fear. Persistent human rights violation, torture and 'disappearances' were no longer the means of social control. Death squads ceased to operate and people could now sleep at night free from fear of being raided by the National Guard.

The open prisons

Given the brutalities perpetrated by the National Guard on their own prisoners, the treatment they received after their defeat in 1979 is exemplary, and indicative of a genuine desire to reunite a people torn apart by civil war. Despite the pressing demands of national reconstruction and development for such a poor country, efforts were made to transform the brutal prison system inherited from Somoza. The aim was to enable prisoners to be productive and encourage a sense of social responsibility. In 1981 over 3,000 ex-National Guardsmen and others convicted of crimes under Somoza worked on the cotton harvest with minimal supervision. This successful experiment led to the setting up of the first open prison, housing 50 National Guardsmen in a farm on the outskirts of Managua. There were no walls and no armed guards, just two wardens. Since the farm opened in 1982, 76 inmates have been released and only five have escaped. An Irish psychologist who is investigating the

Dianna Melrose

Prisoners, including ex-National Guardsmen from the Somoza era, in the leather workshop of the semi-open El Zapotal prison near Managua.

Fiona MacIntosh

A former National Guardsman involved in pig-rearing at the first open prison, 23½km from Managua. Taken shortly before his release.

success of Nicaragua's open prison system in rehabilitating ex-prisoners into the community, has found less than 15% recidivism.[31]

The majority of prisoners are of course still kept in conventional jails, but any prisoner is now eligible to be considered for a place on one of the six open or semi-open prisons, where prisoners are involved in rearing animals, crop production, leather and artwork. Many learn new skills and their families receive some benefit from what they produce. Oxfam has contributed towards the cost of the shower-block in the first open prison and the setting up of its chicken farm.[3] The entire system is built on trust as prisoners can go out on home visits or to buy materials for the workshops, often carrying large sums of money. The prisoners also participate in decision-making through a Prisoners' Council which covers discipline, educational and cultural activities and production.

Obstacles to development

In summing up developments in Nicaragua after 1979, a report by the Inter-American Development Bank concluded that: "Nicaragua has made noteworthy progress in the social sector, which is laying a solid foundation for long-term socio-economic development".[33] Oxfam has witnessed the great steps forward, particularly in literacy, health and community organisation. But it has not, of course, been possible to break completely with the legacy of the past, as Oxfam's Field Director reported in 1983: "The immediate needs of the population are still very considerable. Consciousness is still low that underdevelopment cannot be wiped out overnight and that the answer lies in collective rather than individual solutions. Individualism and a survival mentality are the products of decades of gross repression and grinding poverty. Nicaraguans want their problems as well as their achievements to be seen for what they are, and understood in the context of a small republic constructing its own independent history for the first time this century, precisely when the international correlation of forces could not be more hostile to their efforts".[34]

The initial impressive progress did not go unhindered by violence. Even during the 1980 Literacy Crusade, a number of young *brigadistas* were killed by the *Contra* (counter-revolutionaries), many of them members of the defeated National Guard. In 1981 the effects of these attacks were already beginning to disrupt the Adult Education Programme, as local people had to be mobilised for defence and many became reluctant to go out after dark in areas where the *Contra* were most active.[35]

Increasingly the war began to paralyse long-term health work, such as the training of traditional midwives in the northern border zone.[36] A pattern began to develop in which those most active in community development were victims of selective kidnapping and murder. The growing threat to Oxfam project-holders became reminiscent of the Somoza era.

3. Development Under Fire

CASTILLO NORTE is a State farm 60km from Jinotega in the key northern coffee-growing area. On 15 May 1984 the *Contra* forces launched a devastating attack on this farming community, leaving 21 people dead. The victims included three babies from Miskito families recently resettled there because of fighting elsewhere. At the time the attack started, a visiting Ministry of Health doctor was innoculating the children against polio.

Olivia de la Vides Mesa, a 24-year-old mother, reconstructs what happened at Castillo Norte: "The *Contra* attacked us at 11 am. I was in the kitchen. They began with mortars. There were about 600 of them. We only had 20 militia. One of the mortars fell and killed an old woman in the shelter. When they got nearer, my little sister begged them: 'You already killed an old woman, please don't kill our children'. But they tortured and slit the throats of our militia. I know, because there were so few and they had no more ammunition, they gave themselves up with their hands in the air. And when I got out, they had castrated one of the boys, and cut another's tongue out. And a militia girl who was 4 months pregnant, they raped her and cut off her breasts while she was still alive. They left them all naked. Then they burned them. About 20 *campesinos* were kidnapped".

Benigna Sequeira, local representative of the National Women's Association, reflects: "It's just like the past. They want to come back and do the same

Miskito workers outside the remains of their homes on the *La Sorpresa* State coffee farm within days of a *Contra* attack, November 1984. The wooden superstructure of the houses has been burnt down, leaving them homeless.

27

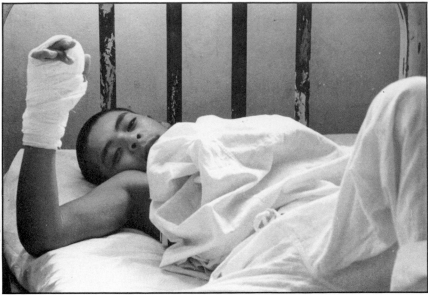

Fiona MacIntosh

A 16-year-old recovering in Jalapa Hospital after being fired at by the *Contra* during an incident on the border.

as in the past. They say the Sandinistas are bad and they want to blame them. They want to bring panic and terror and put the people against the revolution. The children are frightened of the *Contra.* We've already been in another ambush, on April 13 during Holy Week at Las Brisas. There were about 500 *Contra.* They burned our houses and smashed our dishes. We lost everything. Seven of us escaped. One of my children was killed".[1]

In parts of the country, ambushes are common. On 27 July 1984, a truck taking 20 people from Waslala to Matagalpa was attacked. Juan Quinones, a 34-year-old farmer, was in the truck. "It was around 7.30 am about 5km from Waslala. After the *Contra* attack, they forced us to go on to Matagalpa with all the dead and injured, even though Matagalpa was hours away and Waslala would have been much closer. About 1km down the road, we came across another group of *Contra*, about 100 of them. They made us prisoners in the truck, dead and injured and all, for about two hours. They told us we could not leave until they gave the orders. Once they let us go, we went to Matagalpa hospital. I live in Chinandega now. My farm is in Waslala. I'm a working man. I came to see about my animals because my farm's been abandoned. I was in another ambush on my farm in Waslala. The *Contra* took two of my workers, they killed one, the other is in hospital. Those *Contra* keep on killing working people — civilians. They won't let us work. They took all my cattle. The *Contra* have a camp in the mountains. The worker who was killed ran and he hit a mine."[2]

The *Contra* include members of Somoza's still hated National Guard, who form the leadership of the Nicaraguan Democratic Force (FDN) which operates from Honduras, in the north. Recently the FDN have spread to the south, where another *Contra* faction — the Costa Rican-based Democratic Revolutionary Alliance (ARDE) — has been most active. There are also disaffected Miskitos, Sumus and Ramas within the *Contra* ranks. In all, there are estimated to be about 15,000 counter-revolutionaries. Proportionately, it would be equivalent to Britain facing attack and sabotage from more than a quarter of a million terrorists.[3]

They have received substantial backing from the United States Administration and CIA.[4] Ostensibly, this support was first given to the *Contra* for them to help interdict shipments of arms from the Sandinistas to the guerrillas fighting in El Salvador, although no evidence has been presented to prove any shipments taking place. Before taking office in January 1981 and more recently, President Reagan has made no secret of his desire to see the Sandinista Government fall.[5]

In the two years up to the end of 1984, over 7,000 Nicaraguan civilians were killed by the *Contra*.[6] Individual leaders and community organisers who have worked hardest to improve the lives of the poor have been prime targets of the *Contra*. By 1981 Oxfam was receiving a growing number of reports of the systematic killing of project workers, community leaders, health promoters and teachers.

Miskito re-settlement programme

The *Contra* military build-up escalated from the beginning of 1981, with 96 separate border incidents reported between January and April. The level of attack led to the evacuation of isolated communities along the border, who were moved inland for their safety. In January 1982 the Nicaraguan Government took the highly controversial decision to move the Miskitos from their settlements along the River Coco. The Miskitos understandably resented the suddenness of their removal and the loss of their homes and crops, which were destroyed to prevent their being used by the *Contra.* About 10,000 Miskitos fled north across the border, some of them subsequently joining the counter-revolutionary forces.

Whilst criticism must be made of the handling of the situation, Oxfam feels that genuine efforts were made to help the 8,000 or more Miskitos who were resettled inland. In contrast to the totally inadequate resettlement provisions made for the Miskitos 20 years before, the Government took steps to try to provide the five new settlements at Tasba Pri with housing, agricultural and public health services. Immediately after the evacuation, Oxfam made a small grant to buy essential drugs for displaced Miskitos at Tasba Pri, together with emergency grants for Miskitos who had fled to Honduras and ended up in the Mocorón refugee camp.[7] Subsequently, with British Government and EEC co-funding, Oxfam embarked on longer-term projects to provide the new settlements with water pumps and latrines, and continued health education work previously supported along the River Coco.[8]

These and other social development and agricultural projects, both in the new Miskito settlements and on the Atlantic coast in general, have run into a particular set of difficulties. They can be traced to continuing infrastructural

John Howard

The drinking water system installed for 130 Miskito families at Wasminona, one of the five resettlement areas in Tasba Pri. This has since stopped working, partly because of diesel shortages on the Atlantic coast following the *Contra* attack on oil storage tanks at the port of Benjamín Zeledón in October 1983.

problems, especially the lack of roads and transport on the Atlantic coast and the low levels of participation and community organisation. These structural problems on the Atlantic coast have been compounded by the paralysing effects of escalating *Contra* attacks.

In May 1983 a British water engineer, employed by Oxfam, who was coordinating the installation of the new water pumps at Tasba Pri, was fired at while driving between two Miskito settlements. Because of the risk of further attack, he had to be withdrawn before all the pumps were working and before having time to ensure that the Miskito communities understood how to carry out maintenance on the pumps. The problems on the Atlantic coast grew with a new spate of *Contra* attacks on economic targets, including the blowing up of fuel storage tanks in the port of Benjamín Zeledón in October 1983. The resulting acute oil shortages on the coast meant, for example, that there was no diesel to run those pumps at Tasba Pri which were working. So the Miskitos were left without clean drinking water for months.[9]

Disruption of development work

The *Contra* war is wreaking havoc with development schemes all over Nicaragua. Health care has been severely disrupted. For example, in April 1984 a force of about 350 members of the FDN attacked the Miskito settlement of Sumubila. Seven Miskitos (children amongst them) were killed, 14 were wounded and 39 kidnapped including the doctor and two nurses.[10] As reported in *The Lancet,* the impact on the control of infectious diseases is particularly serious: "Several anti-malarial workers and many volunteers have been killed by *Contras.* Their disruption of the health system and communications, and attacks on peasants, have resulted in new malaria problems. It appears that only a termination of hostilities will make it possible for the border areas to achieve the successes in malaria control noted in the rest of the country".[11]

In some cases, development projects are being held back because key organisers are needed to join defence patrols. Leadership training and pig production projects set up at Tasba Pri have been disrupted in this way by the long absence of three out of five trainers and administrators.[12] There has been similar disruption to the Francisco Rivera Veterinary Training School and Chiltepe dairy farm, set up on the outskirts of Managua to increase milk production and improve breeding and veterinary skills. When Oxfam's Field Director last visited the school, all the students were absent because they had been mobilised for defence.[13]

The disruption and human suffering caused by the violence is enormous. By November 1984, almost 143,000 people had been forced to leave their homes.[14] The impact of this man-made disaster and the scale of human need is graphically reflected in the dramatic switch in Oxfam project-funding from development to disaster relief. The table overleaf shows that, whereas between 1980/81 and 1982/83 on average 90% of Oxfam funds went to long-term development projects, in 1983/84 over half its funding had to be channelled into emergency relief. The trend continues and shows every sign of escalating in 1985.

Oxfam project-funding in Nicaragua: 1980–1984

Year	Development (as % total)	Emergency/Humanitarian (as % total)
1980/81	86.5	13.5*
1981/82	96.5	3.5
1982/83	85.5	14.5
1983/84	46.5	53.5
*Humanitarian only, no emergency 1980/81.		

In responding to this need, Oxfam works closely with the National Emergency Committee of the Social Welfare Ministry, which organises emergency food and shelter and longer-term resettlement in collaboration with the unions, community associations and other Government Ministries. Oxfam is just one of many foreign agencies contributing to the huge cost of emergency relief and resettlement, which had reached US$37.5 million by the end of 1983.

The final months of 1983, after the US invasion of Grenada, were a critical time, with widespread fears of full-scale invasion and huge demands on the emergency services as a result of *Contra* attacks. In Rio San Juan on the Costa Rican border, 2,755 people were made homeless and in urgent need of food, clothes, blankets and health care, as were a further 962 displaced people in Zelaya Norte near the Honduran border. The *Contra* attack on the oil storage tanks in the port of Corinto in October left 3,000 people without shelter,

Dianna Melrose

Families resettled in the new Oxfam-supported Jorge Salmerón Cooperative near Chinandega following *Contra* attacks on their homes in the port of Potosí at the beginning of 1984.

followed within days by an attack which devastated an agricultural community in the Pantasma valley, 60km north of the town of Jinotega.

Pantasma came under mortar attack from a force of about 200 *Contra*. In 13 hours' fierce fighting they killed 47 people, most of them peasant farmers. Six teachers were burnt to death inside the Ministry of Education building. The offices, machinery and grain silos of six cooperatives were wrecked, together with the local State-owned coffee warehouse, three basic food distribution centres and numerous vehicles. The saw-mill, which had provided jobs for many local people, was completely wrecked, and 678 people were left homeless.

Oxfam had been poised to provide assistance to the refugees from Corinto, but their needs were being catered for by generous offers of international aid. So funds were made available for food, medicines, clothing, tools, kitchen equipment and housing materials for the people of Pantasma to begin rebuilding their homes and cooperatives.[15]

Resettlement of displaced people

The bulk of the cost of resettlement is housing and construction materials. In the hot, humid province of Rio San Juan more than half the population had been moved or forced to flee from their homes by May 1984. Many refugees were living under makeshift black plastic covers, so new zinc sheeting was provided to keep them dry.[16]

Efforts are made to resettle people displaced by the fighting in new cooperatives, such as the Jorge Salmeron cooperative in Chinandega. At the beginning of 1984 its 70 members and their families were forced to abandon their homes in the northern port of Potosí, after repeated *Contra* attacks. With help from the Ministry of Social Welfare (INSSBI) and the Agriculture Ministry,

Dianna Melrose

"Unity is our greatest strength, today and always "stresses Alfonso Matute (left) of the Jorge Salmeron Cooperative.

33

they selected land and planted maize, cassava, rice, cotton, sorghum and bananas. They dug a well and now share a school and health post with a neighbouring cooperative. Reflecting on the major disruption to their lives and their hopes for the future, Alfonso Matute, one of the lynchpins of the cooperative, stresses: "Unity is our greatest strength, today and always".[17]

Local communities have been able to pull together to help refugees from the fighting who have poured into the towns. In May 1984, for example, an exodus of 898 women, children and old people from cooperatives near the Honduran border arrived in the town of Condega. An emergency committee was immediately set up by the local branch of the Women's Association. Most of the refugees were taken into people's homes and a further 150 were given shelter in a local school. Oxfam's Field Director, who visited Condega within days of the refugees' arrival, was impressed by the way in which peasant families, with little enough themselves, came forward with food and clothes for the refugees who had lost everything when the *Contra* set fire to their homes and cooperatives. The refugees' resilience was evident from their strong desire to get back to their land and start again.[18]

According to the head of technical cooperation at INSSBI, good community organisation has helped to save lives. When the huge oil tank in Corinto exploded after the attack on the port, fire quickly enveloped other tanks containing solvents and molasses. The air was thick with toxic fumes. Families living near the port were in imminent danger from further explosions. In what could have been chaos, the local neighbourhood groups succeeded in

Jenny Matthews

The coffee harvest in Matagalpa, November 1984. The 'soldier' is in fact a civil servant who normally works as an analyst for the water authority, but has been called up to help protect the coffee pickers from *Contra* attacks while they harvest this crucial export crop.

organising the evacuation of 515 families whose homes were close to the tanks, helped by individuals and businesses who volunteered their vehicles.[19]

Economic costs of the fighting

The intensity of attacks and the scale of sabotage of key economic targets has grown. (See p. 38.) This destruction and production losses in 1984 alone cost an estimated US$255 million, equal to over half the estimated export earnings that year.[20]

Each year the aggression has peaked during the key coffee harvest season, beginning in November, in an apparent attempt to destabilise Nicaragua's agriculture-based economy. This harvest is critical because coffee exports alone account for about one-third of Nicaragua's foreign exchange earnings. Attacks have included sabotage of vehicles, processing and storage facilities, kidnapping and murder of agricultural workers and agronomists. Towards the end of 1984, 60 State farms and about ten cooperatives were being attacked each month by *Contra*.[21] Because of the threat to thousands of peasants and young volunteers working on the coffee harvest, Oxfam was asked the previous year to provide first aid kits for the health *brigadistas* who work alongside the coffee-pickers.[22]

Tragically, the effects of the war are now affecting the lives of all Nicaraguans to some degree, through direct attack, military call-up for national defence, higher prices, chronic shortages of food and imported commodities, and breakdown of public and private transport. 90% of the most important basic foods (rice, beans, maize and sorghum) are produced in areas seriously affected by the fighting.[23] The war is fuelling a vicious circle: agricultural production is disrupted, so foreign exchange earnings fall. This makes it impossible to import all the spare parts, tyres and agricultural inputs vital to ensure next year's harvest.

For Nicaragua's poor majority, the *Contra* war poses a direct and growing threat to hopes for a better future. It is a senseless diversion from the real war against poverty and underdevelopment. Nicaraguans who have invested time and effort in setting up schools and cooperatives have suffered the morale-sapping experience of having to start all over again once these have been destroyed.

The imperative of defending the country from attack is now draining a massive 40% of Government funds.[24] Inevitably, the poorest are worst hit by the diversion from development to defence and, as long as the war continues, there will not be time, energy or funds to focus on long-term solutions to the escalating economic crisis that threatens the living standards of the poor.

Ordinary Nicaraguans live in constant fear of *Contra* attacks. This family at the San Luís resettlement camp near Somoto have already suffered, having been forced to leave their home on the Honduran border. Their father is keeping watch while the new school is being built.

THE COST OF AGGRESSION

Since 1982, 3,346 children and adolescents killed by the *Contra,* and 6,236 children have lost one or both parents.

1984

1,500 armed encounters
4,000 *Contra* casualties
3,000 *Contra* deaths

1,000 Nicaraguan army deaths
600 Nicaraguan civilian deaths
2,400 Nicaraguans wounded or abducted by the *Contra*

On average, more than four deaths each day in 1984.

170,000 displaced people (March 1985).

Areas most affected (Number of refugees as percentage of total in May 1984)

Nueva Segovia, Madriz & Esteli (Region 1)   25%
Jinotega & Matagalpa (Region 6)   21%
North Zelaya (Special Zone I)   20%
Rio San Juan (Special Zone III)   13.5%
Chinandega & León (Region 2)   11%
South Zelaya (Special Zone II)   9.5%

About half the population displaced in Rio San Juan; one in three in North Zelaya.

EDUCATION (1984)

98 adult education teachers killed

171 adult education teachers kidnapped

15 primary teachers killed and 16 kidnapped

14 schools destroyed

840 adult education centres closed

354 schools closed

HEALTH

18 doctors and nurses, including two Europeans, killed since 1981.

19 health centres in North Zelaya forced to close since 1981.

7 health centres destroyed in Region 1, and ambulances from Ocotal and El Jicaro ambushed and destroyed.

4 health centres totally destroyed in Region 6, and 9 out of action because of danger to staff.

Delays in finishing 7 new health posts, the Matagalpa Regional Hospital and in starting construction of 15 more health posts in Region 6.

Sources: The Nicaraguan Ministries of Social Welfare, Health and Education.

LOST PRODUCTION
AGRICULTURE
US$75 million losses to May 1984, including basic grains and export crops. 8% of basic grains storage destroyed.

FISHING
59% of fishing boats out of action (destroyed, diverted to defence or no spares).
5 fishing boats sunk by mines, 6 stolen and 2 burnt out.
US$10 million lost shrimp and lobster exports.

FORESTRY
US$6 million lost timber exports.
Important forestry projects in war zones disrupted.

MINING
Gold and silver production in 1983 down 11% on previous years (lack of spares and disruption).
1984 production of Siuna and Bonanza mines on Atlantic coast affected by energy shortage, following attack on El Salto dam.

DAMAGE TO INFRASTRUCTURE
Attack on port of Corinto, October 1983, destroyed 1.6 million gallon oil tank — fire spread to other diesel and solvent storage tanks — 26,000 evacuated.

Air attack on international airport, Managua, September 1983, traffic control tower and airport building damaged.

Port of Benjamin Zeledon attacked October 1983, 2 fuel storage tanks destroyed.

Port Sandino attacked September 1983 and oil pipelines destroyed — repairs estimated at US$330,000.

El Bluff Port mined and storage tanks attacked, February 1984.

Mining of Ports, damages estimated at over US$9 million by May 1984. After a complaint by Nicaragua the International Court of Justice issued a preliminary ruling that: "The United States of America should immediately cease and refrain from any action restricting, blocking or endangering access to or from the Nicaraguan ports, and in particular, the laying of mines," followed by a statement in November 1984 that, despite US objections, it has jurisdiction to pursue Nicaragua's complaint.

Bridge over Jiguina River, Jinotega dynamited August 1983, along with others in the north-west.

Construction Ministry site on Matagalpa-Waslala road attacked June 1983, with destruction of 30 vehicles (worth US$1.8 million) and damage to plant of US$300,000.

Electric Power Lines in Region 4 sabotaged, December 1983. Repairs over US$1 million.

Source: INSSBI

Note: This catalogues some of the major losses. It is by no means a comprehensive list of attacks or damage.

4.Debt,Trade and Aid

IF THERE WERE NO counter-revolutionary aggression, Nicaragua would still face very serious problems. All five Central American countries have been severely hit by the combined effects of world recession, debt crisis and the increasingly hostile terms of trade with the industrial nations. In Central America these structural inequalities between North and South are compounded by the political and military conflict that divide the region, disrupting trade and economic growth.

By the end of 1983, real incomes in Costa Rica, Guatemala and Honduras had fallen to the levels of the early 1970s. In Nicaragua and El Salvador, the two countries most severely affected by war, real wages have plummeted to the levels of the early 1960s.[1] Whereas its four neighbours' economies all suffered negative growth, Nicaragua had a growth rate of 5% in 1983, representing a slight recovery after the dramatic falls in production that accompanied the overthrow of Somoza.[2] Moreover, of central importance to the poor (in terms of prices of basic necessities), the cost of living in Nicaragua was the lowest in the region.

But, with the economy increasingly driven onto a war footing and inflation now running at over 50%, Nicaragua's economic prospects are bleak. In June 1984, the deteriorating economic situation forced the Government to end food subsidies, except those on milk and sugar. More recently, all food subsidies have had to be stopped, which presents a serious threat to the nutrition of the poorest.

All the Central American States are struggling against similar problems, with falling commodity prices, trade barriers, and cuts in the availability of long-term credit. Nicaragua faces a particularly hostile climate because opposition from the Reagan Administration has affected its access to international finance, development aid and export markets.

Debt

By comparison with the big Latin American debtors (Mexico, Brazil and Argentina) Nicaragua's foreign debt is minute. But for such a poor country the US$3,500 million debt is equivalent to 7.5 times its total estimated export earnings in 1984.[3]

Ironically, Nicaragua's indebtedness dates back to Somoza who, as President, ran up a debt of US$1,640 million and fled leaving reserves of only US$3.5 million. Generous loans to the dictatorship failed to benefit the people in any way, including an IMF credit of US$32.2 million paid into the Central Bank in June 1979, which 'disappeared' weeks later with Somoza.[4] The new Government took responsibility for the debt it inherited. Since then, with the rise in interest rates and new borrowing for reconstruction and development, the national debt has risen steeply.

Interest payments alone cost over 43% of Nicaragua's export earnings in 1982, falling to 20% of export revenue the following year after the short-term debt had been successfully renegotiated.[5] But the debt problem still looms large. Towards the end of 1984, the World Bank cut off a US$2 million loan to improve Managua's water supply because Nicaragua had fallen 90 days behind in some of its debt repayments. In 1985, the Government must begin paying back capital from the Somoza debt renegotiated in 1980.[6]

Nicaragua stands alone amongst its Central American neighbours in refusing to enter into an agreement with the International Monetary Fund (IMF). IMF 'medicine' (which generally includes sharp cuts in public spending) tends to hit the poor hardest, so it runs directly counter to Nicaragua's development priorities.[7] Because it has not entered into an agreement with the IMF, Nicaragua's access to credit from other official and private banks is effectively blocked. However, the deteriorating economic situation and the cost of the war have now forced the Government to freeze public expenditure as part of a package of austerity measures announced in February 1985.[8]

Trade

Factories in Nicaragua have had to grind to a halt because of the foreign exchange crisis. Towards the end of 1984 more than half the trucks used to transport food in and out of Matagalpa province in the north, and half the capital's buses, were off the road for want to tyres and spare parts — many of which can only be obtained from the United States with hard currency.

Underlying the acute shortage of foreign exchange is Nicaragua's growing trade deficit, which stood at over US$500 million in 1983. Exports that year were down one-third of 1977, and almost twice as much was paid out for imports as the total earned on exports.[9]

This reflects both the huge demand generated by reconstruction and development and the sharply deteriorating terms of trade for non-industrialised, non-oil-exporting countries like Nicaragua. Commodity prices fell in 1982 to their lowest US dollar levels since World War II.[10] Nicaragua's four main exports have all been badly hit.

Dianna Melrose

Chronic shortages of imported spare parts are having a disastrous impact on transport. An overcrowded bus broken down on the road between Chinandega and León, September 1984.

Prices paid for Nicaragua's export commodities (in US$)

	Peak Year	1983
Coffee	(1977) 184.8	106
Cotton	(1981) 75	64
Sugar	(1981) 23.4	13.5
Meat	(1980) 130	100

Prices per 100 lbs (1 *quintal*) from major buyers.

Source: *National Reconstruction Government of Nicaragua, Economic Policy Guidelines 1983–1988.*

The problems of fluctuating and falling prices are, of course, shared by the vast majority of developing countries which are heavily dependent on exports of a few commodities. The only long-term solution lies in diversifying their economies to reduce this dependence, and establishing commodity agreements with developed countries to help stabilise prices and guarantee access to their markets. Nicaragua has the added difficulty of political differences with the United States, traditionally the main market for Nicaraguan produce, including sugar bought at subsidised prices. In 1983, the United States cut the sugar quota by 90%, forcing Nicaragua to find alternative markets in Algeria, Mexico and the USSR. But the United States remains a major customer for Nicaraguan exports, especially bananas, seafood and meat, despite a threatened ban on imports of Nicaraguan meat in 1984 by the US Department of Agriculture on health grounds.[11]

In common with other developing countries, Nicaragua suffers as a result of trade barriers erected by developed countries to protect their industries. Each year it loses millions of dollars by exporting bales of unprocessed cotton, only to re-import expensive thread and finished clothing. In sharp contrast to lower returns on unprocessed commodities, prices of oil and manufactured goods have risen steeply. Whereas in 1970 a 100lb bag of Nicaraguan coffee bought 100 barrels of oil, the same bag was only worth three barrels by 1982.[12]

About one-third of Nicaragua's growing import bill has been used to pay for oil, which was supplied until recently under a Mexican-Venezuelan credit facility. This has been suspended because of late payments, so Nicaragua is now having to barter commodities for oil from the Soviet Union. The high cost of imported energy has made the development of alternative energy resources a high priority, and one of the biggest schemes now under way, mainly with finance from Italy and other European countries, is a geothermal project to tap the power of the Momotombo volcano, near Managua.

Aid

The new growth-orientated economic strategy to create self-sufficiency and social development can only be achieved through large-scale aid and finance from abroad. The World Bank estimated in 1981 that Nicaragua would need approximately US$125 million in 'soft' loans (long-term credit at very low interest) by 1982/83.[13] In the event, credits from the World Bank's soft loan affiliate, the International Development Association (IDA) fell far short of this amount, as did credit at nearer-commercial rates from the International Bank for Reconstruction and Development. (IBRD).

World Bank Loans to Nicaragua

	IBRD	IDA
1979	—	—
1980	**20**	**32**
1981	**33.7**	**5**
1982	**16**	—
1983	—	—
(Source: *Hansard,* 15.12.83).		

Nicaragua is not the only developing country to have suffered since the IDA's major funder, the United States, began cutting back the Bank's provision for soft loans.[14] But the Reagan Administration has made a number of overt attempts to block credit to Nicaragua from multilateral banks. In 1983 it voted against a US$34 million Inter-American Development Bank (IADB) loan to revitalise Nicaragua's fishing industry. This loan was in fact agreed, but funding from the main multilateral agencies, including the World Bank, all but dried up after 1982. More recently, in January 1985, the US Secretary of State

The Momotombo Volcano and geothermal wells. The steam-driven generator should produce a fifth of Nicaragua's electricity needs and save on the high cost of imported oil.

George Shultz is reported to have urged the IADB to block a US$150 million loan to Nicaragua. This would have provided credit to small and medium producers to boost basic food production.[15]

The first signs of economic boycott came early in the Reagan Administration with the cutting off of credit for wheat purchases from the United States in March 1981. US economic aid to Nicaragua of US$36 million in the final year of the Carter Administration, was cut to US$3.1 million in 1981, and completely suspended from the end of 1982. By contrast, US economic and military aid to Costa Rica, Honduras and El Salvador was substantially increased.[16] Moreover, the US Administration has lobbied to dissuade other countries from giving aid to Nicaragua. In September 1984, George Shultz is reported to have written to EEC Foreign Ministers before their San Jose meeting urging them to ensure that European aid policy to Central America "does not lead to increased economic aid or any political support for the Sandinistas".[17]

By 1982, private investment in Nicaragua had slumped to 10% of total investment, compared with 80% in 1978. Moreover, an estimated US$766 million worth of private assets have been taken out of the country since 1978.[18] But in keeping with the commitment to a mixed economy, over three-quarters of total agricultural and industrial production remained in private hands.[19]

Nicaragua has, however, been successful in generating loans and aid from a wide range of countries. Between 1979 and 1984, these totalled over US$2,489 million. Over two-thirds of bilateral loans were from other Latin American, non-aligned or Western countries.[20]

Sources of aid to Nicaragua 1979 — March 1984

Multi-lateral	**25%**
International	28%
Regional	72%
Bilateral	**75%**
Western Europe	14%
North America	4.5%
Latin America	41%
Africa & Asia	7.5%
Socialist countries	33%
Source: UN Report A/39/391 15 August 1984.	

With the cutting back of funds from the multilateral agencies, the gap has partly been made up by increased aid from Eastern European countries, which rose from 32% of total aid before 1982 to 41.5% in 1983. But aid from Western Europe increased more significantly from 12% to 25% of total aid in 1983.[21]

Non-government aid

Non-governmental organisations of many nations have made a considerable contribution to Nicaraguan development programmes estimated at more than US$50 million over the past five years. Oxfam's aid, and that of similar organisations, is increasingly channelled through the Augusto César Sandino Foundation (FACS), a non-governmental agency created in 1981 to channel international NGO aid to small-scale community development projects.

The International Reconstruction Fund (FIR) coordinates foreign funding for government development projects in agriculture, industry, energy, transport and social infrastructure. Current and planned projects require external funding of almost US$1,500 million.[22] The sheer scale of Nicaragua's development needs are thus well beyond the scope of voluntary agencies. This means that major aid donors such as Britain have a vital role to play in assisting future peaceful development in Nicaragua.

5. The Role of Britain and Europe

UK Bilateral Aid

BRITAIN gave substantially more aid to Nicaragua during the five final years of the Somoza dictatorship than during the first five years of the Sandinista Government. From a high point in 1977, at a time when opposition to the dictatorship was becoming universal, British bilateral aid has fallen sharply since 1979. (Table 1).

Britain's annual bilateral aid contribution is now roughly two pence for every Nicaraguan, compared with about sixteen pence in 1977. This cutting back of official aid to Nicaragua contrasts sharply with the positive experience of British voluntary agencies. It is also hard to reconcile with stated priorities to maximise the use of limited aid funds which include:

(1) Former UK colonies or dependencies

As a former British dependency, Belize received most British aid per head in Central America, equivalent to just under £41 in 1983. (Table 2) Nicaragua and Honduras both have distant historical links with Britain, dating back to the 19th Century Mosquito Kingdom Protectorate along the Atlantic coast. Yet Honduras receives substantially more aid than Nicaragua.

(2) A concentration on the poorest 50 countries

No Central American country falls within the World Bank's category of the poorest 50 countries.[1] But Costa Rica, with a gross national product per head 1.5 times greater than Nicaragua's, was allocated almost 40 times more UK aid per person in 1983. (Table 2)

(3) ". . . a greater focus of aid resources . . . where local policies seemed likely to be supportive of aid efforts . . ."[2]

On this criterion alone, in the experience of British voluntary agencies, the case for increased bilateral aid to Nicaragua would seem compelling. Nicaragua's positive development approach has been singled out for praise by a variety of international agencies. For example, in the journal of the British Overseas Development Administration an article on a US$70 million loan to Nicaragua from the International Fund for Agricultural Development concludes that "no other IFAD loan had reached its target group so rapidly and relatively efficiently".[3]

A UK Government Minister has acknowledged "Nicaragua's good record in the spending of development aid", and the British Chargé d'Affaires accredited to Managua in 1984, readily conceded that Nicaragua has a "very impressive record on social development", and an "amazing" one in comparison

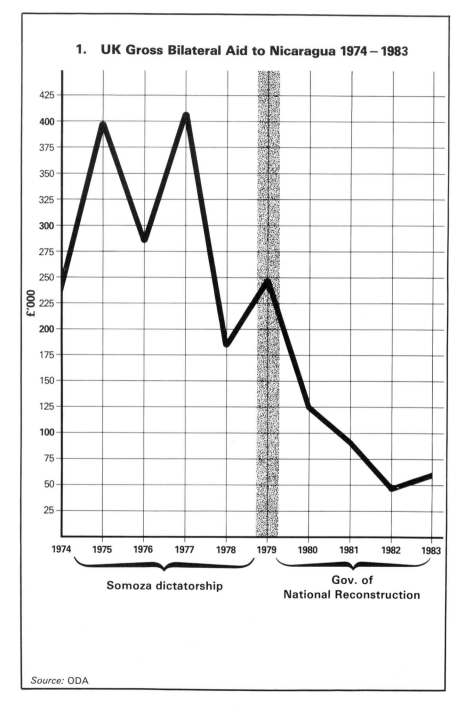

1. UK Gross Bilateral Aid to Nicaragua 1974 – 1983

£'000

Somoza dictatorship

Gov. of
National Reconstruction

Source: ODA

46

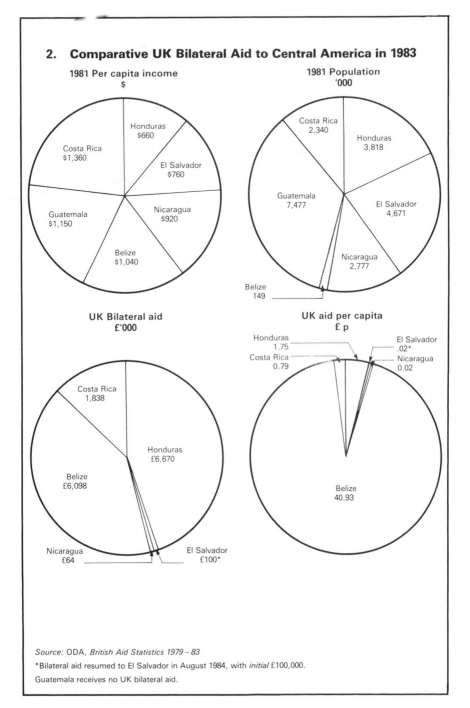

2. Comparative UK Bilateral Aid to Central America in 1983

1981 Per capita income $

- Honduras $660
- El Salvador $760
- Costa Rica $1,360
- Nicaragua $920
- Guatemala $1,150
- Belize $1,040

1981 Population '000

- Costa Rica 2,340
- Honduras 3,818
- Guatemala 7,477
- El Salvador 4,671
- Nicaragua 2,777
- Belize 149

UK Bilateral aid £'000

- Costa Rica 1,838
- Honduras £6,670
- Belize £6,098
- Nicaragua £64
- El Salvador £100*

UK aid per capita £ p

- Honduras 1.75
- El Salvador .02*
- Costa Rica 0.79
- Nicaragua 0.02
- Belize 40.93

Source: ODA, *British Aid Statistics 1979 – 83*

*Bilateral aid resumed to El Salvador in August 1984, with *initial* £100,000.

Guatemala receives no UK bilateral aid.

47

with El Salvador and Honduras.[4] Honduras is, however, currently receiving £6.6 million of British aid — over 100 times more than Nicaragua. (Table 2)

(4) ". . . a greater focus of aid resources on those sectors where it was felt there was a need for assistance . . ."[5]

In 1984 Britain resumed bilateral aid to El Salvador with the decision to reintroduce a technical cooperation programme and immediate aid of £100,000 for "urgently needed civilian supplies and equipment".[6] Yet, according to the Foreign Office, El Salvador is already the "sixth largest recipient of US bilateral aid in the world".[7]

Honduras and Costa Rica are also large-scale beneficiaries of US economic aid to Central America which totalled US$1,100 million in 1984.[8] Moreover these two countries have received large sums of British bilateral aid for major development projects. In 1983, the Commonwealth Development Corporation put up £1 million to improve the water supply in Costa Rica, and £3 million for oil palm development and energy projects in Honduras.[9]

Despite its pressing reconstruction and development needs, over the past five years total British aid to Nicaragua (£458,500) amounts to only a 7% of aid to Honduras in 1983 alone.[10] (The figure for UK aid to Nicaragua for 1984 has not yet been officially published but, according to the ODA, amounts to £25,000 — excluding the UK contribution of £41,379 in 1984/85 to the in-country expenses of eleven CIIR volunteers.)

The inescapable conclusion from the apparently inconsistent allocation of UK bilateral aid to different Central American countries is that aid to Nicaragua is being judged on a different set of criteria. Moreover, parliamentary records reveal UK Government objections to Nicaragua of an essentially political nature.[11]

In fact the British Government gives no direct aid to the Nicaraguan Government. The miniscule bilateral aid programme amounted to only £64,000 in 1983. This was used to fund three scholarships, the costs of six British CIIR volunteers working in Nicaragua and small-scale development projects co-funded with Oxfam, Christian Aid and CAFOD. UK aid funds channelled through Oxfam have helped to support basic food production, water supplies for the open prison and Miskito settlements, and miners' safety equipment.[12]

Because there are ample opportunities for positive development work in Nicaragua, and following the recommendation made by the All-Party Foreign Affairs Committee in 1982 that "efforts be made to increase the present very low level of political, economic and cultural relations between the nations", Oxfam, Christian Aid and CAFOD made a joint request to the Minister of Overseas Development for £150,000 to be shared between the agencies over two years.[13] But this unprecedented joint agency approach for a relatively modest sum was turned down.

Oxfam receives over £1.5 million from the Overseas Development Administration (ODA) each year to co-fund projects worldwide. In July 1984 the ODA circulated new procedures for administering the Joint-Funding Scheme. Nicaragua appeared on a new list of 21 countries where "for a number of different reasons ODA is required to obtain prior clearance".[14] Subsequently the list was withdrawn, but political vetting of Nicaraguan projects through the Foreign Office continues.

Other European Aid Donors

Britain stood alone in Europe, alongside the United States, as the only major aid donor to give less aid to Nicaragua in 1982 than a decade earlier. (Table 3) In recent years the Netherlands has been the largest bilateral aid donor to Nicaragua, providing technical assistance and soft loans worth almost US$24 million in 1982. (Table 3) Dutch economic assistance has been very flexible, allowing Nicaragua to buy vital spare parts from United States suppliers. Spain has also been an important source of credit (totalling US$84 million up to June 1984) which could be used to purchase inputs and perishables, as well as capital goods and services.[15]

Bilateral aid from France, Sweden and West Germany in 1982 dwarfed Britain's contribution. (Table 3) The French mainly gave wheat as food aid. Sweden provided soft loans and technical assistance in forestry, mining and financial administration. Italy, Denmark, Belgium and Ireland have given relatively small amounts of aid but have taken a more positive diplomatic approach to Nicaragua. Finland, which has almost no tradition as an aid donor, is now providing substantially more aid to Nicaragua than Britain. West Germany, which was the largest European donor in 1979–80, has since cut back its aid and excluded Nicaragua from its initial 1985 aid provision.[16]

EEC Aid

Within the EEC, the British Government has voiced strong political objections to increasing aid to Nicaragua. Answering a parliamentary question in November 1982, a Government spokesman said: "In considering who should benefit we have to take account of the low priority which the Government of Nicaragua appears to give to using resources for social and economic development, as well as their curbs on civil rights, the treatment of minorities, and the continuing military build-up in Nicaragua".[17] That month, the EEC Foreign Affairs Council decided against allocating a proposed special aid package to Nicaragua. But France and other member States argued successfully for additional funds to be allocated without discrimination against Nicaragua.[18]

In fact, Nicaragua did relatively well from the EEC between 1980 and 1983, receiving on average one-third of the total EEC aid to Central America. (Table 4)

The EEC is also involved in co-funding projects in Nicaragua through European voluntary agencies. Surprisingly, in 1984 two relatively small projects that Oxfam proposed to the EEC were turned down without any objection to them being made on development criteria. One project was for a chicken farm at the open prison for ex-National Guards, to which UK bilateral aid funds had previously been contributed.[19] The other project that the EEC rejected was to improve facilities at a training school used by members of local community groups (known as *Comites de Defensa Sandinista*) to improve their organisational and communication skills.[20]

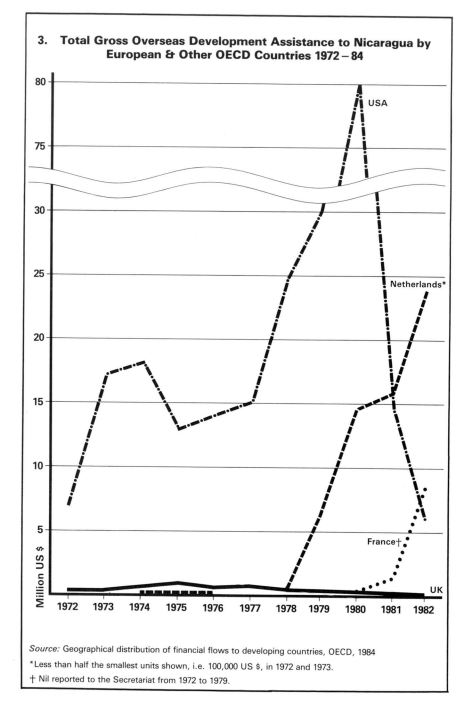

3. **Total Gross Overseas Development Assistance to Nicaragua by European & Other OECD Countries 1972 – 84**

Source: Geographical distribution of financial flows to developing countries, OECD, 1984

*Less than half the smallest units shown, i.e. 100,000 US $, in 1972 and 1973.

† Nil reported to the Secretariat from 1972 to 1979.

4. Total EEC Aid to Central America
(%)

	1979	1980	1981	1982	1983
Guatemala	0.7	0.6	0.5	1.0	3.8
El Salvador	2.5	5.7	10.4	4.9	5.4
Honduras	26.4	28.4	10.9	23.6	32.2
Nicaragua	28.0	23.3	50.7	17.6	33.9
Costa Rica	0.6	0.6	0.7	17.2	1.7
Other*	41.8	41.4	26.8	35.7	23.0

Source: Aides CEE à l'Amérique Latin, EEC tables for 1979–1983.
Other includes Mexico, Domican Republic, Haiti, Panama and Regional Programmes.

Before their meeting in San José, the capital of Costa Rica, in September 1984, EEC Foreign Ministers were lobbied by the US Administration not to increase aid to Nicaragua. Since then a British Minister has reassured Parliament that the Government has no intention of "discriminating against an individual country in what is a region-to-region exercise".[21] As a result of the San José meeting an extra US$15 million was to be added by the EEC to its annual aid allocation to Central America of US$30 million.

Trade

But what Europe gives with one hand is taken away by another. The sharp fall in prices paid by European buyers for Central American coffee, sugar and cotton between 1978 and 1982, coupled with the rising cost of European manufactured goods, is estimated to have cost Nicaragua alone US$180 million in 1982.[22]

The extent to which the terms of trade have worked in Europe's favour and against Nicaragua are striking. The cost to Nicaragua of importing chemical products, machinery, transport and other goods from the EEC more than trebled between 1979 and 1983. But Nicaragua's earnings on exports to the EEC have fallen in real terms since 1979. (Table 5)

British trade with Nicaragua is still minimal despite an upsurge in 1984. In fact Britain offers less of a market for Nicaraguan commodities than Nicaragua does for British goods. Moreover UK exports to Nicaragua have fallen sharply since 1978. (Table 6) British trading relations with Nicaragua are also very low in relation to UK trade with other Central American and Caribbean countries (Table 7), and exceptionally small in relation to Nicaraguan trade with France, West Germany and Italy. (Table 8)

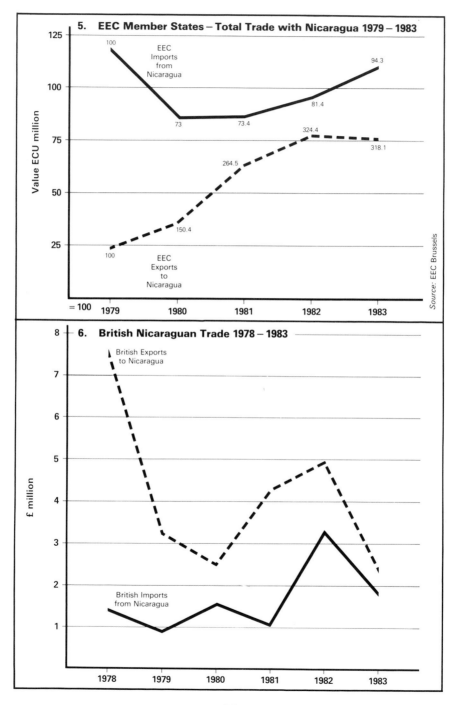

5. EEC Member States – Total Trade with Nicaragua 1979 – 1983

Value ECU million

125

100

EEC
Imports
from
Nicaragua

94.3

81.4

73

73.4

324.4

318.1

264.5

150.4

100

EEC
Exports
to
Nicaragua

= 100

Source: EEC Brussels

1979   1980   1981   1982   1983

6. British Nicaraguan Trade 1978 – 1983

8

British Exports
to Nicaragua

7

6

5

£ million

4

3

2

British Imports
from Nicaragua

1

1978   1979   1980   1981   1982   1983

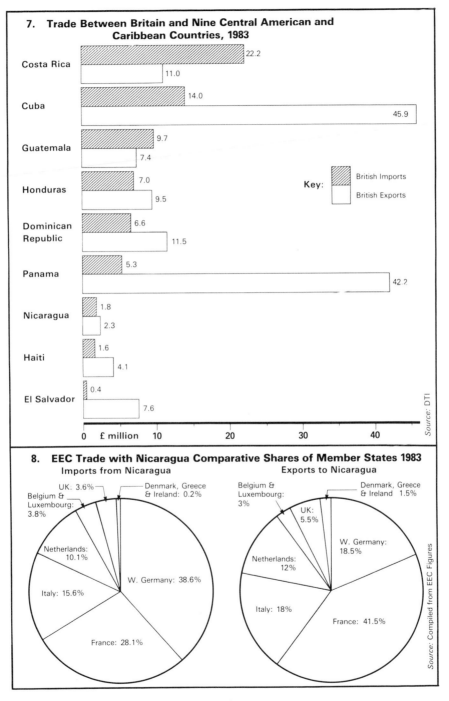

7. Trade Between Britain and Nine Central American and Caribbean Countries, 1983

Costa Rica — British Imports: 22.2, British Exports: 11.0

Cuba — British Imports: 14.0, British Exports: 45.9

Guatemala — British Imports: 9.7, British Exports: 7.4

Honduras — British Imports: 7.0, British Exports: 9.5

Dominican Republic — British Imports: 6.6, British Exports: 11.5

Panama — British Imports: 5.3, British Exports: 42.2

Nicaragua — British Imports: 1.8, British Exports: 2.3

Haiti — British Imports: 1.6, British Exports: 4.1

El Salvador — British Imports: 0.4, British Exports: 7.6

Key:
British Imports
British Exports

0   £ million   10   20   30   40

Source: DTI

8. EEC Trade with Nicaragua Comparative Shares of Member States 1983

Imports from Nicaragua

UK: 3.6%
Belgium & Luxembourg: 3.8%
Denmark, Greece & Ireland: 0.2%
Netherlands: 10.1%
W. Germany: 38.6%
Italy: 15.6%
France: 28.1%

Exports to Nicaragua

Belgium & Luxembourg: 3%
UK: 5.5%
Denmark, Greece & Ireland 1.5%
W. Germany: 18.5%
Netherlands: 12%
Italy: 18%
France: 41.5%

Source: Compiled from EEC Figures

Women workers weeding in the cotton fields on a private estate near León. In many areas the bulk of agricultural work is undertaken by women as the men have been mobilised for defence. Export earnings from cotton have declined with European and other buyers paying lower prices in 1983 than in 1981. Cotton yields were also hit by disastrous flooding in Chinandega and León in 1982.

The sharp fall in UK exports to Nicaragua from 1978 can be traced to the decision to suspend Export Credit Guarantee Department (ECGD) cover in March 1979, at the height of the civil war to oust Somoza.[23] ECGD acts as a Government-backed insurance policy for British exporters against the risk of not being paid for goods sold abroad. It is always stressed that decisions over ECGD cover are taken on purely commercial assessments of risk. The Prime Minister has added in relation to Nicaragua: "We cannot make ECGD cover available for any country failing to meet certain criteria laid down by the World Bank and the IMF in the repayment of its debt".[24] As an ex-Member of Parliament has pointed out: "The bitter irony . . . is that the Government refuses to assist Nicaragua's economic recovery, including ECGD help, because it was the Somoza regime that ratted on its obligations".[25]

Apart from the fact that the people of Nicaragua are left to pay for Somoza's borrowing which did nothing to improve their lives, the Nicaraguan case points to the wider inadequacies of institutions like the ECGD. As now constituted, the ECGD is hardly effective in promoting trade with developing countries. It assesses 'risk' on the basis of the country's foreign exchange position; most Third World countries are desperately short of foreign exchange, which is precisely why British Government action is needed to facilitate credit for essential goods and services. Moreover, institutions like the IMF are primarily concerned with short-term liquidity to the exclusion of long-term social and economic development that benefit the poor majority.

A longer-term view and more equitable trading policies, including commodity agreements to help to ensure a fair return for Nicaragua's exports, would benefit Nicaraguans who need goods that Britain can produce. This would also be in the interests of British people who need jobs. From the perspective of a European diplomat in Managua, there would be opportunities to sell more British goods if the British Government took a long-term view. Nicaragua's rail stock, for example, is urgently in need of replacement, and a new railway is planned from the port of Corinto to Managua and eventually to the Atlantic port of El Bluff at Bluefields. British Rail and private contractors could do with orders.

Dianna Melrose

An obsolete engine at the railway station in León. New rail stock is urgently needed as well as other goods which could present export and job opportunities in Britain.

In the critical area of finance, Britain and other European countries could greatly assist long-term development and stability in Nicaragua by increasing its access to soft loans. This would help Nicaragua pursue an independent foreign policy without any need for increased dependence on the Eastern bloc.

A POLITICAL SOLUTION

Contadora

To improve the lives of the Nicaraguan people the immediate priority must be to stop aggression by the *Contra*. Currently, the main framework for achieving a negotiated solution to the war in Nicaragua is the 'Contadora' peace initiative, which seeks to resolve wider tensions and conflict in the region as a whole. This peace initiative takes its name from Contadora Island, off the coast of Panama, where officials of four Latin American countries — Colombia, Mexico, Panama and Venezuela — first met in January 1983 to talk about the Central American crisis. Since then, the 'Contadora' group of countries has held a series of meetings with Government representatives from Costa Rica, El Salvador, Guatemala, Honduras and Nicaragua, the five Central American countries directly affected.

A statement of joint objectives has been drawn up. These include the need to halt the arms race in the region, reduce stocks of weapons, end foreign military involvement in the region (through withdrawal of foreign bases and military advisers), control arms traffic and prevent national territory from being used to destabilise the governments of other Central American countries. The 'Contadora' objectives also include the need for all States to make a commitment to social and economic development, popular participation in decision-making, democratic pluralism and national reconciliation.[26] The difficulties that loom ahead are to get the different countries to agree on concrete implementation of these proposals, including verification of arms reductions and withdrawal of foreign military advisers.

The 'Contadora' talks are important because they are a Latin American attempt to achieve a political solution and end foreign intervention in Central America. Moreover, 'Contadora' has widespread support including that of governments and parties across the political spectrum in Western Europe. At present there is no viable alternative. But the obstacles are enormous, not least the fact that 'Contadora' can get nowhere without backing from the United States because of its heavy involvement in the region.

When a draft treaty emerged in 1984, Nicaragua was the first Central American country to state its readiness to sign. This courted the immediate displeasure of the Reagan Administration which interpreted the Nicaraguan move as a pre-electoral publicity coup.[27] Since then, despite Nicaraguan claims to want tighter arms control provisions in the draft treaty, the 'Contadora' negotiations have temporarily faltered with the cancellation of talks scheduled for February 1985. Bilateral talks between the Americans and Nicaraguans, described as vital by the British Government, were also broken off by the US Administration. But Nicaragua has shown a readiness to negotiate by agreeing to withdraw 100 Cuban advisers and reduce arms purchases, leaving the way open for further talks.

Europe's Role

Without a political solution, Nicaraguans will continue to suffer and die. As war cripples the economy further, the poorest will be the worst hit. There is a real risk of a serious escalation in the regional conflict, with possible implications for US commitments to NATO and European defence.

The British Government has repeatedly stressed its support for the 'Contadora' initiative as representing the best hope for achieving peace and stability in Central America.[28] The Government has also endorsed the consensus European view that "the problems of Central America cannot be solved by military means, but only by a political solution springing from the region itself and respecting the principles of non-interference and inviolability of frontiers".[29]

But at the same time, the British Government sits perilously on the fence by continuing to express support for US policy objectives in Central America.[30]

Hardliners in the Reagan Administration quite openly support the *Contra* and their military action to "prevent consolidation" of the Sandinista Government.[31] Uncritical faith in the US charges against Nicaragua may account for inconsistencies in British Government statements. The Foreign Minister, for example, stated in the Commons on 20 July 1983 that "there is *clear evidence* of a Soviet-Cuban-Nicaraguan link, bringing arms and disruption to the area" (our italics).[32] But within five days his under-Secretary said: "Whilst we have *no evidence* that Nicaragua is directly exporting Soviet arms, we have noted a disturbing increase in military supplies to Nicaragua from the Soviet Union and its allies in recent months" (our italics).[33]

The British Government did denounce the mining of Nicaragua's ports.

Fiona MacIntosh.

Refugees from the fighting — a Nicaraguan family in the resettlement camp near Somoto: until a negotiated settlement to the *Contra* war is reached they cannot return to their home and live in peace.

But, in contrast with France which offered to help clear the mines, Britain stopped short of voting for the UN Resolution condemning American involvement in the mining. The British Government has not protested to the Honduran Government about the *Contras'* use of their territory to launch attacks on Nicaragua, but has been particularly critical of the military build-up in Nicaragua on the grounds that it threatens neighbouring States.[35]

The resolution of conflict in Central America as a whole and the well-being of its people cannot be served by isolating Nicaragua further from its neighbours. Instead the British Government could use its diplomatic skills to help to draw Central American countries together and to encourage serious peace negotiations. Good groundwork has been made with a British Chargé d'Affaires in Nicaragua, and increased diplomatic contact with Nicaraguan and other Central American Ministers. Within Europe, the British Government is uniquely well placed to exert a positive influence on US thinking because of its close relationship with the Reagan Administration.

Despite the obstacles, the desire of the Nicaraguan people is clear. The conflict must be stopped and European support is urgently needed to help to promote peace and development.

6. Action for Change:
Summary and Recommendations

"La solución somos todos" ("We are all part of the solution").
Nicaraguan development worker.

Summary

SINCE THE FALL of Somoza the Nicaraguan people have made impressive achievements in social development. The Nicaraguan positive development approach, based on meeting the needs of the poor majority, is now being increasingly undermined by the *Contra* war to destabilise and isolate Nicaragua. Nicaraguans are suffering both as a result of direct military aggression and growing economic crisis. Within Europe, Britain should play a more constructive role in actively promoting an end to *Contra* aggression and the right of Nicaraguans to self-determination.

The following recommendations arise from Oxfam's experience in Nicaragua. They are based on action that the Nicaraguans themselves would like Britain and the EEC to take to help to end the war and contribute to long-term peaceful development.

RECOMMENDATIONS
The British Government should:

1. Exert its influence with the governments of the United States, Central American and 'Contadora' group countries to bring an immediate end to the *Contra* war.

2. Take an active role, with its EEC partners, in pushing for implementation of the 'Contadora' proposals by promoting constructive talks between Nicaragua and the United States, and Nicaragua and neighbouring countries.

3. Increase bilateral aid to Nicaragua to a comparable level with Honduras and assess aid to Nicaragua solely on development criteria.

4. Use its influence as a major contributor to the World Bank and other multilateral agencies to ensure that there is no political discrimination against Nicaragua in the allocation of loans.

5. Restore Export Credit Guarantee Department (ECGD) cover to facilitate trade between Britain and Nicaragua.

6. In the long term, give serious attention to the need for commodity agreements with non-Lomé countries (like Nicaragua) to help to stabilise prices, guarantee access to markets and a fair return on raw materials.

The EEC should:

1. Give more active political support to a negotiated settlement of conflict in the region and full implementation of the 'Contadora' proposals.

2. Increase development and emergency aid to Nicaragua.

3. Judge aid applications for Nicaragua solely on development criteria.

4. Take concerted action to facilitate soft loans to Nicaragua and improve the terms of trade through commodity agreements.

Notes and References

NOTE: In references where a number is prefixed by NIC (eg. Chapter 1. Note 7: NIC 6) this indicates Oxfam's internal project reference. Details of some of these programmes may be obtained from: The Information Dept., Oxfam House, 274 Banbury Road, Oxford OX2 7DZ, UK.

Chapter One

1. World Bank, *World Development Report 1984,* pp. 218–219.

2. CIDCA, *Trabil Nani*, Historical Background and Current Situation on the Atlantic Coast of Nicaragua,* Report of the Centre for Research and Documentation of the Atlantic Coast (CIDCA), 1984, pp. 6–7. *Miskito for "Many troubles".

3. Project DP 3292, Oxfam Grants Lits 1963/64.

4. Projects NIC 1 and NIC 2, Oxfam Grants Lists for 1968–69, 1969–70 and 1971–72.

5. Project 7221, vaccine for polio epidemic (up to £5,000), Oxfam Grants List 1967–68.

6. Project 3 CRS. Also CIDCA, op. cit., p.61.

7. Emergency grants NIC 6 (1972/3).

8. Project NIC 13, National Youth Movement legal aid clinic (1977/8).

9. Collins J., with Moore Lappé F. and Allen D., *What Difference could a Revolution Make? Food and Farming in the New Nicaragua,* Institute for Food and Development Studies, 1982, p.89.

10. The voluntary agency is *Instituto de Promoción Humana* (INPRHU), Oxfam project holders (NIC 6, 12, 20). Oxfam support to the Los Arcos Cooperative between 1976 and 1982 included salaries of two health visitors and one agriculturalist, credit, seeds, fertilisers, and medicines (NIC 7).

11. Projects NIC 8 and 9.

12. Project NIC 10 (1977/8).

13. Project NIC 16 — grants of £17,560 in 1978/9.

14. Project NIC 13.

15. *The Central American Crisis: A European Response,* Transnational Institute, Amsterdam 1984, p. 15. For a full account of the insurrection see Black G., *Triumph of the People. The Sandinista Revolution in Nicaragua,* Zed Press, 1981.
Also *Whitakers Almanac 1985,* population of City of Birmingham 1,011,000.

Chapter Two

1. World Bank, *World Bank Report, 1983,* p.5.

2. Ibid, p. 5.

3. Council on Interracial Books for Children , "Education for Change: A Report on the Nicaraguan Literacy Crusade." in *The Nicaraguan Reader,* Rosset P. & Vandermeer J. ed., New York 1983, pp. 335–336. Also Ministerio de Educación, Nicaragua, *5 Años de Educación en la Revolución 1979–1984,* Managua, July 1984, pp. 47–54.

4. Ministerio de Educación, 1984, op. cit. pp. XVII and 52.

5. Project NIC 22.

6. Ibid.

7. Ibid.

8. Project NIC 13.

9. Ministry of Education Nicaragua, *5 Años de Educación en la Revolución, 1979–84,* op. cit., p. XVII.

10. Ibid., p. XVII.

11. "Developments in Health Care in Nicaragua", *New England Journal of Medicine,* Vol. 307, No. 6, 5 August 1982, p. 389.

12. Health Ministry Nicaragua, *Documento Base,* Ier Congreso Nacional, *Journadas Populares de Salud,* 20.2.84, p. 27.

13. Project NIC 35.

14. Health Ministry Nicaragua, op. cit. pp. 7, 12. *New England Journal of Medicine,* 1982, op. cit., p. 389.

15. Letter to *The Lancet* 17.9.83. from L. J. Bruce-Chwatt, Wellcome Museum of Medical Science.

16. *New England Journal of Medicine,* op. cit., p. 389.

17. Table: *"Indicadores Demográficos y de la Situacion de Salud 1977–83".* Source: División Nacional de Estadística e Informática, Ministerio de Salud. Also, UNICEF, The State of the World's Children 1985 (UK coverage 1982: polio 78% and measles 50%), p. 117.

18. Project NIC 32.

19. CIDCA, 1984, op. cit.

20. Laurence Morris, CIIR volunteer, in interview with the author, September 1984. Project NIC 70.

21. Collins J., op. cit., p.89.

22. Projects NIC 20 and NIC 20A.

23. Projects NIC 24.

24. Collins J., op. cit. p.39.

25. *"Reforma Agraria: Síntesis de Titulaciones"* table from CIERA, 1984.

26. "Los Pequeños y Medianos Productores Agropecuarios", Union Nacional de Agricultores y Ganaderos (UNAG), 1983, p.2.

27. Project NIC 41.

28. Instituto Histórico Centroamericano, *Envio,* July 1984.

29. "Evolución de la Producción Alimentaria 1977/78 — 1983/84" table compiled by CIERA.

30. Per capita consumption of basic foods, table compiled by CIERA.

31. Benny McCabe and Capt. Raul Cordón, Director of the Nicaraguan National Penitentiary System, in interview with the author, September 1984.

32. Projects NIC 42 and NIC 54.

33. IADB Report No. DES-13, *Nicaragua,* January 1983.

34. Oxfam internal memorandum, 8.2.83.

35. Project NIC 22.

36. Project NIC 32.

Chapter Three

1. Testimony from Oxfam project-holder, Sister Mary Hartman, Human Rights Commission. Also report on Castillo Norte attack from National Emergency Committee of INSSBI.

2. Ibid.

3. *The Economist,* 2.3.85. "15,000 *Contra* attacking a population of 3 million would be equivalent proportionately to Britain's population of 55 million under attack by 275,000."

4. McConnell J., "Counter-revolution in Nicaragua: the US Connection", *The Nicaraguan Reader,* Ed. Rosset and Vandermeer, 1983, pp. 175–189. Also Gutman R., "America's Diplomatic Charade", *Foreign Policy* No. 56, Carnegie Endowment for International Peace, Fall 1984, pp. 3–23.

5. State of the Union address 6.2.85, quoted in *Herald Tribune,* 14.2.85.

6. National Emergency Committee, *48 Meses de Agresión Extranjera, una Exposición de Denuncia y Análisis,* Año II No. 4, INSSBI, 25.12.84, p.7.

7. Project NIC 37. Also Project Honduras 30 — emergency grant of £20,000 for water storage at Mocoron refugee camp.

8. Projects NIC 39 and NIC 40.

9. Project NIC 39.

10. INSSBI, op. cit.

11. *The Lancet,* 19.5.84, p. 1125.

12. Project NIC 44.

13. Project NIC 74.

14. INSSBI, op. cit., p. 7.

15. Project NIC 68.

16. Project NIC 73.

17. Project NIC 53.

18. Oxfam internal memorandum, 5.6.84.

19. Miriam Lazo, INSSBI, in interview with the author, September 1984.

20. *Financial Times,* 10.1.85.

21. Instituto Histórico Centroamericano, *Update* No. 41, 27.11.84, p. 2.

22. Project NIC 69.

23. "Distribución es Clave", *Pensamiento Propio,* Instituto de Investigaciones Económicas y Sociales and Coordinación Regional de Investigaciones Económicas y Sociales, 15.7.84, p. 28.

24. President Daniel Ortega, quoted in *Herald Tribune,* 11.2.85.

Chapter Four

1. CEPAL. *Centroamerica: Evolución de sus Economiás en 1983,* 30.3.84. quoted in *Pensamiento Propio.* May/June 1984, pp.19–24.

2. Ibid., p. 19. Also ECLA.

3. *Herald Tribune,* 23.10.84. Estimated export earnings in 1984 US$461 million.

4. "The Somoza Legacy: Economic Bankruptcy", EPICA Task Force, in *The Nicaraguan Reader, Documents of a Revolution Under Fire,* Ed. Peter Rosset and John Vandermeer, 1983, p. 300.

5. *Pensamiento Propio,* op. cit. Also *Envio,* No.37, July 1984.

6. *Herald Tribune,* 23.10.84. Also *Financial Times* 10.1.85.

7. Latin America Bureau, 1983, *The Poverty Brokers — The IMF and Latin America.*

8. *The Times* 11.2.85. Also *The Guardian* 11.2.85.

9. CEPAL in *Pensamiento Propio,* op. cit., pp. 21–24.

10. World Bank, *World Development Report 1983, p. 11.*

11. *Herald Tribune,* 23.10.84.

12. Moore Lappé F. and Collins J. *Now We Can Speak: A Journey Through the New Nicaragua,* IFDP, 1983, p. 4.

13. World Bank Report on Nicaragua, 1981, *The Challenge of Reconstruction.*

14. Overseas Development Institute Briefing Paper 3.9.84., *The World Bank: Rethinking its Role.*

15. Central American Historical Institute, *US-Nicaraguan Relations 1981–1984,* p. 32. Also National Reconstruction Government of Nicaragua, *Economic Policy Guidelines* 1983–1988, pp. 5, 9, 35. Also, *The Guardian,* 9.3.85.

16. PACCA, *Changing Course, Blueprint for Peace in Central America and the Caribbean,* IPS, 1984, pp. 114–116.

17. *Herald Tribune,* 1.10.84.

18. *Envio* No. 37, July 1984.

19. IADB Report on Nicaragua, No. DES–13, July 1983.

20. United Nations General Assembly, *Assistance to Nicaragua, Report of the Secretary General,* A/39/391, 15.8.84, p. 3.

21. Ibid., p. 3.

22. National Reconstruction Government of Nicaragua, *Economic Policy Guidelines 1983–1988,* op. cit., Annex 1, p. 2.

Chapter Five

1. World Bank, *World Development Report 1984,* p. 218.

2. Overseas Development Administration (ODA), *United Kingdom Memorandum to the Development Assistance Committee, 1984.*

3. ODA, *Overseas Development,* June 1982.

4. Letter from Baroness Young to Oxfam Director, 27.12.84. Also Richard Owen, in interview with the author, 14.9.84.

5. ODA, 1984, op. cit.

6. ODA Press Release, 14.8.84.

7. Foreign and Commonwealth Office UK, background brief, *Crisis in Central America,* August 1983, p. 3.

8. *Herald Tribune,* 9.1.85.

9. ODA, *British Overseas Aid, 1983,* p. 22.

10. Ibid. Also letter from Baroness Young to David Atkinson MP, 3.12.84. British aid is also provided for refugees through contributions to the International Committee of the Red Cross (ICRC) (£400,000 in 1983/4) and the UN High Commissioner for Refugees (£200,000 in '83/84).

11. *Hansard:* 20.7.83. Sir Geoffrey Howe, 20.7.83. Cranley Onslow, 28.7.83. The Prime Minister, 19.3.84. Timothy Raison, 12.12.84. Tim Renton, 20.12.84. Baroness Young.

12. ODA, *British Overseas Aid, 1983.* Also Projects NIC 20, NIC 39, NIC 42, NIC 70.

13. *Foreign Affairs Select Committee Report on Central America and the Caribbean,* HMSO December 1982, para. 255.

14. ODA, *The Voluntary Agencies Joint-Funding Scheme, Memorandum of Understanding on Block Funding Arrangements for Oxfam,* June 1984.

15. Central American Historical Institute, *Update 46,* January 1985.

16. *Fondo Internacional de Reconstrución* (FIR) officials in interview with the author, September 1984.

17. *Hansard,* 16.11.82, Cranley Onslow.

18. *Hansard,* 20.12.82. Also European Community, *External Relations,* No. 908, 1982.

19. Project NIC 54.

20. Project NIC 67.

21. *Hansard,* 20.11.84, Baroness Young.

22. CEPAL, *Notas Para el Estudio Económico de América Latina, Nicaragua,* E/CEPAL/MEX/1983/L.13, quoted in Government of Reconstruction, *Economic Policy Guidelines, 1983–1988,* op. cit., p. 8.

23. *Hansard,* 21.12.82.

24. Letter from Mrs Thatcher to Judith Stinton, 2.1.85.

25. *Hansard,* 2.3.82., Stanley Clinton Davis.

26. UN Security Council Document S/160 41 *The Situation in Central America: Note by the Secretary General,* Annex *Document of Objectives,* 18.10.83, pp. 4–6.

27. *The New York Times,* 24.9.84.

28. *Hansard,* 12.12.84.

29. Stuttgart Declaration, Document A 021/6, Folio 65.

30. For example *Hansard,* 25.7.83.

31. Fred C. Ilke, Under Secretary of Defence, quoted in *The Nicaragua Reader,* op. cit., p. 25. Also R. Gutman, "America's Diplomatic Charade", *Foreign Policy* No. 56, Fall 1984 and President Reagan quoted *The Economist* 2.3.85.

32. *Hansard,* 20.7.83.

33. *Hansard,* 25.7.83.

34. *Hansard,* 27.6.84. A decision taken on the grounds of the wording of the resolution.

35. *Hansard,* 25.7.83.

Abbreviations

AMNLAE   Asociación de Mujeres Nicaraguenses Luisa Amanda Espinoza — Nicaraguan Women's Association.

ATC   Asociacion de Trabajadores del Campo — Farm Workers' Association.

CAFOD   Catholic Fund for Overseas Development.

CDS   Comité de Defensa Sandinista — Sandinista Defence Committee.

CIDCA   Centro de Investigaciones y Documentación de la Costa Atlántica — Research and Documentation Centre for the Atlantic Coast.

CIERA   Centro de Investigaciones y Estudios de la Reforma Agraria — Agrarian Reform Research and Study Centre.

CIIR   Catholic Institute for International Relations.

CRS   Catholic Relief Service.

ECLA   Economic Commission for Latin America.

EEC   European Economic Community.

ENABAS   Empresa Nicaraguensa de Alimentos Básicos — Nicaraguan Basic Foodstuffs Enterprise.

FACS   Fundación Augusto César Sandino — Augusto César Sandino Foundation.

FDN   Fuerza Democrática Nicaraguense — Nicaraguan Democratic Force.

FIR   Fondo Internacional de Reconstrucción — International Reconstruction Fund.

FSLN   Frente Sandinista de Liberación Nacional — Sandinista National Liberation Front.

LADB   Inter-American Development Bank.

IBRD   International Bank of Reconstruction and Development.

IDA   International Development Association.

INPRHU   Instituto de Promocion Humana — Institute for Human Advancement.

INSSBI   Instituto Nicaraguense de Seguridad Social y Bienestar — Nicaraguan Institute of Social Security and Welfare.

MIDINRA   Ministerio de Desarrollo Agropecuario y Reforma Agraria — Agricultural Development and Agrarian Reform Ministry.

PACCA   Policy Alternatives for the Caribbean and Central America.

UNAG   Unión Nacional de Agricultores y Ganaderos — National Farmers' and Ranchers' Union.

UNCTAD   United Nations Conference on Trade and Development.

WUS   World University Service.

Further Reading

Black, George, *Triumph of the People: The Sandinista Revolution in Nicaragua,* Zed Press, London, 1981.

Collins, Joseph with Moore Lappé and Allen, *What Difference Could a Revolution Make? Food and Farming in the New Nicaragua,* Institute for Food and Development Policy, San Francisco, Revised edition, 1985.

Rosset, Peter, and Vandermeer, John, ed. *The Nicaragua Reader: Documents of a Revolution under Fire,* Grove Press, Inc., New York, 1983.

Walker, Thomas W., Ed., *Nicaragua in Revolution,* Praeger, New York, 1982.

Policy Alternatives for the Caribbean and Central America, *Changing Course: Blueprint for Peace in Central America and the Caribbean,* Institute for Policy Studies, Washington, 1984.

Holland, Stuart, and Anderson, Donald, *Kissinger's Kingdom: A Counter-Report on Central America,* Spokesman, Nottingham, 1984.

Black, George, and Bevan, John, *The Loss of Fear: Education in Nicaragua Before and After the Revolution,* Nicaragua Solidarity Campaign and World University Service, London, 1980.

Lappé, Frances Moore, and Collins, Joseph, *Now We Can Speak: A Journey Through the New Nicaragua,* Institute for Food and Development Policy, San Francisco, 1983.

Pearce, Jenny, *Under the Eagle: US Intervention in Central America and the Caribbean,* Latin America Bureau, London, 1982.

Barry, Tom; Wood, Beth, and Preusch, Deb, *Dollars and Dictators: A Guide to Central America,* Zed Press, London, 1983.
Kornbluh, Peter, *Nicaragua: The Price of Intervention,* Institute for Policy Studies, Washington, 1985 (forthcoming).

The Central American Crisis: A European Response, Transnational Institute, Amsterdam, 1984.

Comment: Nicaragua, Catholic Institute for International Relations, London, 1984.